The Immortal Imagination:

THE 22ND NORTH CAROLINA INFANTRY REGIMENT IN WAR AND PEACE

JOHN SHEEHAN

KEITH MILLMAN

The Immortal Imagination:

THE 22ND NORTH CAROLINA INFANTRY REGIMENT IN WAR AND PEACE

The Immortal Imagination

THE 22ND NORTH CAROLINA INFANTRY REGIMENT

ESSAYS & PHOTOGRAPHS BY

JOHN SHEEHAN

KEITH MILLMAN

DEDICATED TO THE MEN AND WOMEN OF

The 22nd North Carolina Infantry Regiment

PAST AND PRESENT

M.T. Publishing Company, Inc.™

P.O. Box 6802, Evansville, Indiana 47719-6802
WWW.MTPUBLISHING.COM

Copyright © 2016
John Sheehan & Keith Millman
All rights reserved.

Library of Congress Control Number: 2015958374

ISBN: 978-1-938730-87-0

Prepress & Publishing by
M.T. Publishing Company, Inc.™

Contents

INTRODUCTION

2013 marked the 150th anniversary of the Battle of Gettysburg, the battle that many regard as the turning point in the American Civil War. In three days of fighting in July 1863, and at a collective cost of over 50,000 casualties, the scales of the Civil War tipped inexorably in favor of the North, and as a result, the democratic values that have come to be known as "traditionally American" were both preserved and strengthened in that field of blood. From June 27-June 30, 2013, a commemorative re-enactment of the battle took place on this hallowed ground.

At this re-enactment, John Sheehan, a historian and author at Tompkins Cortland Community College (TC3) in New York, and Keith Millman, a photography professor at TC3 and established photographer, embedded with, interviewed, and photographed--with period "tintype" technology--a Southern unit-- the 22nd North Carolina Infantry Regiment. During this time embedded within the unit, accoutered in period clothing graciously provided by our hosts, Keith produced the labor-intensive tintypes using authentic equipment, while John marched, drilled, carried the colors, and fought with the unit, in order to share their "experiences" with them, and later interviewed these re-enactors to determine their motivations for re-enacting. These contemporary tintypes and biographies have been matched with archival biographies of the men from the original regiment that fought at and survived, or died in, this horrific, but decisive, sacrifice at Gettysburg.

The purpose of this book is to deepen the connection between contemporary Americans and their historic past for educational purposes. The American people are a product of their history, their shared and evolving stories, and the reality of those stories in their lives today. Men and women today, and the re-enactors who portray the sacrifices of those who have gone before, those who ultimately re-united and saved this nation, need to be remembered and celebrated. The re-enactors who portray those who fought and died for their states and their newly-declared country, even in defiance of the principles fostered by their opponents, need to have their stories told, so that young people today can assess for themselves the path, and the costs of that path, to the hard-won "American" values that can so easily be taken-for-granted today. Young people need to be part of this celebration in ways that will be relevant to them. The photographs, the biographies of the re-enactors, and the biographies of the Civil War soldiers at Gettysburg will together help give new breath and relevance to this story, and thus makes this a project worthy of fruition. This is what the idea of "Living History" is all about. We, the authors, believe that this project will be a valuable legacy that will help further this goal.

Human beings are social creatures. We are cultural creatures. We are not born with social ideas in our heads. The views of "our people," the views we have been enculturated to, become our personal views, which we imbibe uncritically. Often, we are unaware of this sociological fact. This project will delve into the identity of the "American" people. Who is an American, and more importantly, what are the values that a typical American holds to be true? The American Civil War hammered those values out on the anvil of sinew, blood, and courage. From the crucible of Gettysburg, the American "heart" was re-forged. As educators, John and Keith believe that students today are uninformed, or seriously under-informed, on these issues, how these issues were resolved, and how these issues nonetheless form the very foundations of each student's core beliefs. It is necessary to bring the events, and their results, of the Civil War, in general, and the Battle of Gettysburg, in particular, to their collective consciousness. Utilizing old technology in a new way, when coupled with the biography of a modern American re-enactor and the biography of a Civil War soldier, will link the idea of what it means to be an American across the generations. It will make relevant the notion that we Americans are a people that re-invent ourselves generationally, but that re-invention is always grounded upon core values.

Americans are a people whose ideals are enshrined in the ideals of "freedom" and "sacrifice" for the common good. These ideals are not communicated well enough today. The notion of freedom, and the foundational rights that buttress it, have come to connote an acquisitive, self-serving identity, rather than a community-serving, sacrificial one. The survivors and the dead of Gettysburg, and the re-enactors who keep their spirits alive today are worthy of being highlighted in this project that is aimed at re-leavening our youth, the carriers of our ideals into the future, with an understanding of what traditional American values are. The values of diversity and inclusion were tempered in fire on the fields of Gettysburg. The values of "We the people" have been steadily forged in the halting steps of a people addressing the needs of centuries of evolving political thought, economic practices, and social structures. These lofty goals have always been the beacon that Americans have aspired to in the main, while each generation brings its civically-engaged part in this process to fruition. The holistic sweep of American history has yielded "self-evident" truths that need to be understood in ways that tell the whole story of this great experiment in democracy that is America. This entails looking at each segment in this history diachronically, that is, looking at and analyzing the motivations and social structures as they existed in salient snapshots of time during this nation's history, without seeing the result from hindsight, and then examining the next segment of history through it's own lens, etc., and finally going back and running the thread of a posteriori conclusions through them. This is part and parcel of the idea that underscores sociological thought today, termed the "Sociological Imagination."

This book is a small attempt to be a part of that process, and the authors recognize in advance that the story each generation tells itself in the Great History of the United States is only a generational "myth" that gets re-interpreted and judged by its descendents according to contemporary social "realities." It is also recognized that the typical American is not a homogenized social and political entity. Each of us are local and regional entities, each with his or her own particularly "mythical" viewpoint and political agenda, and that some people, in all regions, will find some of the points and arguments made here tough to swallow; but true democracy is not intended to quiet the voices of those with whom one disagrees in order to hallow one "glorious" mythologized vision, but to listen to the voice of the other as well, and to adjust the political process in a utilitarian way according to the voices of all in this cacophony that is American Culture. This is the nature of the dialectical method, which is the hallmark methodology of Western thought: analyze all evidence in favor of an idea, then analyze all evidence against that idea, and finally synthesize new--relativistically-mythologized "truth." It cannot be otherwise in a government "of the people, by the people, and for the people," and work.

John and Keith would like to thank several people for their invaluable help in the creation of this work: Mathea Millman for assisting with all the photography for this book. Beth Vangasbeck for her tireless efforts in typing and transcription; Craig Carroll, Lance Carroll, and Mark Ragan for providing the authentic uniform and equipment that enabled the field experience to become practicable; Karen Fuller for providing period paraphernalia needed for the encampment, as well as introducing us to Ken Snyder; and Ken Snyder, the Colonel of the 22nd North Carolina Infantry Regiment, who graciously went out of his way to enable this project to become manifest. John and Keith have also resolved beforehand to contribute 50% of their own profits generated from sales of this book to the Wounded Warrior Project.

Re-enacting the American Civil War "began even before the real fighting had ended. Civil War veterans recreated battles as a way to remember their fallen comrades and to teach others what the war was all about. The Great Reunion of 1913, celebrating the 50th anniversary of the Battle of Gettysburg, was attended by more than 50,000 Union and Confederate veterans, and included re-enactments of elements of the battle, including Pickett's Charge. Modern re-enacting is thought to have begun during the 1961–1965 Civil War Centennial commemorations. Re-enacting grew in popularity during the 1980s and 1990s, due in large part to the success of the 125th Anniversary re-enactment near the original Manassas battlefield, which was attended by more than 6,000 re-enactors. In 1998, the 135th anniversary re-enactment of the Battle of Gettysburg took place near the original battlefield. There have been several estimates on the number of participants, but it is widely agreed that it was the largest re-enactment ever held anywhere in the world, with between 30,000 and 41,000 re-enactors participating. This event was watched by about 50,000 spectators. Over 8,000 re-enactors participated in the150th Anniversary re-enactment at Gettysburg." (en.wikipedia.org/wiki/American_Civil_War_reenactment) Why do modern-day men and women invest in, take time off from work to participate in, and talk to spectators at, Civil War re-enactments? Why do the men and women of the 22nd North Carolina Infantry Regiment do so? This book will tell you why by using their own words. First, however, let's read the mission statement of the 22nd North Carolina Infantry Regiment, as written in its website. (www.22ndnorthcarolina.org/about-us/history)

"The Mission of the 22nd North Carolina Infantry Regiment is to honorably portray, as historically as is reasonable, the soldiers of the 22nd North Carolina Infantry Regiment, their uniforms and accoutrements, camp life, hardships, and battle engagements during the period of 1861 to 1865…."

"To accomplish this mission the regiment will engage in Civil War Living History encampments; displays and demonstrations; and participate in Civil War Battle Reenactments…. This regiment will be inclusive as to developing relationships within the Civil War Reenacting community Goals of the 22nd North Carolina Infantry Regiment."

"1. The Goal of the 22nd North Carolina Infantry Regiment is to educate and inform the general public and our selves through research, so that the heritage, hardships, and experiences of the Civil War soldier and civilians of the South can be fully understood and appreciated."

"2. The Goal of the 22nd North Carolina Infantry Regiment will include the development and growth of the regiment through active recruiting without respect to sex, race, religion, age, or national origin, and the building of relationships with other reenacting groups, National Park Services, private businesses, and the public in general."

Other than active recruiting, the mission of the 22nd North Carolina Infantry Regiment, as stated, is to portray the heritage and experience of Southern soldiers and civilians during the Civil War through Living History. To do this, one must also include salient historical and social factors and perspectives before and after the war. This is where Living History comes in. What is Living History?

"Living history (wikipedia.org/wiki/Living_history) is an activity that incorporates historical tools, activities and dress into an interactive presentation that seeks to give observers and participants a sense of stepping back in time. Although it does not necessarily seek to re-enact a specific event in history, living history is similar to, and sometimes incorporates, historical re-enactment. Living history is an educational medium used by living history museums, historic sites, heritage centers, schools and historical re-enactment groups to educate the public in particular areas of history, such as clothing styles, pastimes, handicrafts, and particular skills, or to simply convey a sense of the everyday life of a certain period in history…. Many Americans use the past in their daily lives, while simultaneously viewing the place where they often encounter history – the school – with varying levels of distrust and disconnectedness. Living history can be a tool used to bridge the gap between school and daily life to educate people on historical topics. Living history is not solely an objective retelling of historical facts. Its importance lies more in presenting visitors with a sense of a way of life, than in recreating exact events, accurate in every detail…. Individuals can participate in living histories as a type of experiential learning in which they make discoveries firsthand, rather than reading about the experience of others…. Formal education can help visitors interpret what they see at living history sites. By providing a structured way of looking at living histories, as well as questions to think about during visits, formal education can enrich the experience, just as living histories can enrich learning in the classroom."

As stated in the foregoing definition, Living History is not necessarily a bias-free objective rendering of the "facts." No history is, ever was, or ever will be, truly objective. All points of view are subjective. All documents are subjectively written, and all histories are agenda-driven, however much an author tries to be objective; and I know several good authors that try to do just that. I also know several authors that don't. That is why a democracy must listen to the voices of all, even the one's you don't like. Unsupported opinions are the bugbear of democracy. True scholarship is really a piñata, and indeed should be. Living History is a valuable adjunct to formal teaching either through books or media. It is good to remember that all learning is accomplished under the rubric of the Sociological Imagination. (legacy.lclark.edu/~goldman/socioimagination)

The Sociological Imagination is a concept coined by the noted sociologist C. Wright Mills. The concept was developed in order to help people orient themselves in a given society. That has been the job of a sociologist form the very beginning. As Mills purported, most people, unfortunately, define themselves through, and anchor their identities through, "troubles." Troubles arise when the psychological "conscious" cannot control external events, which gives rise to inner angst. Mills maintained that "in defense of selfhood" in troubling circumstances, people may "become morally insensible." History shows that throughout history people were powerless to effect changes in the structures of their societies that would give them some sense of control over their destinies. Hence, the great experiment in democracy that is the United States. The United States and the meaning given to American democracy is now, and has always been since the birth of the Republic, a peculiarly fascinating ideal, not only to Americans now and in the past, but also to those foreigners who look on American political aspirations with troubled feelings of their own that range from envy and fear to admiration and hope. Democracy offers people the hope of escaping their troubles by proffering them the prospects of being the agents of institutional restructuring and historical change. "The Sociological Imagination "enables its possessor to understand the larger historical scene in terms of its meaning for the inner life and the external career of a variety of individuals…. It is the idea that the individual can understand (his or) her own experience and gauge (his or) her own fate by locating (him or) herself within (his or) her period." People have to discern their own social "realities." What is the structure of this particular society as a whole? Where does this society stand in human history; and what varieties of men and women now prevail in this society and in this period? These "are the questions inevitably raised by any mind possessing the Sociological Imagination." And any scholar plumbing the depths of the Sociological Imagination in a particular social structure must possess "the capacity to shift from one perspective to another, from the political to the psychological…." (pp. 2-3) To embrace the Sociological Imagination of a "true" democracy takes an open mind. It is not an easy thing to do. Alas.

An analysis of the American Civil War from a historical and a sociological perspective reveals how that conflict has shifted in the Sociological Imagination in the United States. Regional and sectional interests were alive and festering long before the conflict erupted into the most violent war the American people has ever known, and rose like a phoenix from the ashes to transform hydra-like into the neo-mythologies that we write about and read about in books and listen to and view in the media and public assemblies today. It is worth learning more about the place of the American Civil War in the Sociological Imagination of Americans, that polyglot group of mixed identities, angsts, and "truths" that both unite and disunite us as a people. Hence, the title of this book--The Immortal Imagination--dances on these ideas, and seeks to explore them in the hope of understanding a few of the fibers that make up the skein of this nation's Sociological Imagination about the importance of the Civil War and the Battle of Gettysburg.

Some of the transmogrifying concepts that have been hallowed in the values of the United States include the ideas of

Freedom, Progress, Rugged Individualism, Manifest Destiny, States' Rights, and Federal Governance. Unlike the Ten Commandments, these ideas have not been carved in stone that stand timeless throughout history. They have been erected, maintained, discredited, hallowed, and demonized in varying ways throughout the vicissitudes of this nation's ever-contingent sense of history. Again, how could it be otherwise. Some claim that the Civil War was entirely about ending slavery based upon scriptural righteousness, both in the Bible and in the Constitution. Ironically, both testaments of the Bible and the antebellum U.S. Constitution uphold slavery as a political and social institution. In fact, some claim that the Blacks were cursed by the biblical deity to perennial slavery because of a despicable act committed by Canaan upon Noah. Others claim that the war was caused by hypocritical and greedy hyper-capitalists denying the ability of gentlemen farmers the right to enrich themselves progressively, by foisting unfair and excessive taxes and tariffs on a non-industrial sector of the national economy, while decrying their unjust social institutions. I say that both are operating under this amorphous social construct of what an "American" is and how that creature thinks. The common denominator that unites these parties is the primal human pursuit of resources necessary to survive, and access to those resources. This is the nature of any and every socio-economic order humans have devised for themselves, right back to the beginning of social organization. The flies-in-the-ointments, of course, are those historical institutions that humans have devised in the justification for political, social and economic inequalities--across the board. Unequal access to resources is just that, unequal, despite any veneer of justification to the contrary. The justifications are the grist of the mill of the Sociological Imagination.

Without arguing too deeply, the historical roots of this nation can be traced back to the ideas of the physiocrats--that is, that all wealth ultimately comes from the land--and the mercantilists--that is, that there is a finite amount of resources contained within that land (and air and water) that can be harnessed and converted into national power, and that any nation/people that can marshal its power most efficiently will be able to expand its power and exert dominion/imperium over its neighbors in a very Hobbesian (dog-eat-dog) world. Fresh water for hydration, running water for power, grains, animals, produce, minerals, air quality, access to trade, a favorable balance of trade, and human beings themselves--whether owners, workers, peasants, or slaves--are all assets in a secular community, where "national interests" transcend the social institutions decreed by a deity. Everything becomes an asset, even such arcane things as "intellectual property." If it is an asset, it can be taxed and translated into power. If one nation couldn't compete with its neighbors with the net value of its assets, then it had to accrue those assets elsewhere to restore "the Balance of Power" in the view of Europeans living during the Early Modern period, when the idea of Civil Rights for national citizens were slowly germinating. Remember, the advent of Human Rights had to await the aftermath of the traumas of World War II in order to try people for "crimes against humanity."

Colonization of the New World made available vast new sources of resources and wealth, and the non-citizen (that is, those with no civil rights) populations necessary to do the mundane task of accruing those resources for the colonizers, in order for the colonizers to ship those resources back to the Mother Country, in order to redress the power imbalances back home, where wars were becoming more and more expensive due to gunpowder technology and scientific acumen harnessed to the needs of the nation. When immunity-bereft local populations/assets succumbed to the ravages of horrific and unknown causes, a result undesired by the colonizers, other populations/assets were bartered for and/or kidnapped from shores that were more immunity-friendly to the burgeoning Atlantic World. The Slave Trade of Blacks and the removal of Natives were "rational" choices acted upon according to the Sociological Imagination of the Machiavellian worldview and the epidemiological factors of the Colombian Exchange. The colonials of the Thirteen Colonies were enculturated into the mores of this worldview, which was a Northern European worldview. Southern Europe, which was the Classical font from which the Northern European worldview had sprung, was a more arid region than Northern Europe, and, on either end of the Mediterranean, abutted the Muslim world in a mutually hostile and mutually exhausting state of conflict. Southern Europe clung to its triune division of medieval Catholic society into Three Estates bent on accomplishing the will of deity in its political processes, while asset-rich Northern Europe evolved into the seemingly oxymoronic, but absolutely "progressive" mercantilistic worldview that could embrace both democracy for national citizens, and slavery for those who were not. It is a Sociological Imagination that seems abhorrent to us today, but that would be a relativistic judgment of history, and cultural others, from our own empyrean perches. In the "progressive" march of democratic values, Civil Rights, those freedoms accruing to citizens within a specified nation-state, preceded universal Human Rights, a global concept that was only comprehensible once European imperialism had successfully leavened the planet with its cultural values. American geography, ironically, would mimic European geography, that is, that a warm southern climate and a temperate northern climate would work on the Northern European Sociological Imagination and cause it to shape-shift and cleave in a typically "New World" landscape.

The Slave Trade was a major asset and coup that (northern European) Great Britain was able to wrest from (southern European) Spain in their several conflicts over the resources of the Atlantic World. When the United States imbibed the fermenting ideology of democracy that was threatening its Mother, and successfully separated from her, in the immortalized American Revolution, the sociological structures--Freedom for Brothers, and Slavery for Others--was already a part of our collective "imagination." It would not remain that way. Temperate northern climes made slavery an economic liability in areas where produce could be grown aplenty, but could not compete with the identical produce grown back in the similarly temperate Mother Country. But, access to the Appalachian Mountain Piedmont rivers provided ready power sources for the mills that were a few score miles from the seaports of the Northern cities and the mineral-rich hinterlands, and enabled the Northern industrialist to compete favorably with British manufacturers. The self-made-man--the Rugged Individual--was the hero of the new Northern Imagination, but he was draped in a merchant's cloak. Geography also kept those self-same power-laden Appalachian rivers hundreds of miles from the coasts of the steamy and mineral-rich Southern climes where semi-tropical crops could be lucratively harvested with intensive manual labor. The self-made-man--the Rugged Individual--was the hero of the new Southern Imagination, as well, but he was outfitted in the garb of a gentleman farmer. The main similarity between the two regions was that successful citizens craved wealth and prestige as a social good; the main differences between the regions were that geography fostered an industrial and wage-earning mentality in the North and an agricultural and slavery-defending mentality in the South. It was agreed that Black slaves would be three-fifths human for political reasons in the infancy of the nation to survive the threats of tough neighbors to the north and south of her borders, British Canada and Spanish Florida. The initial overlaps in the Sociological Imaginations of the citizens of the newly independent United States would ramify with time.

The defeat of Britain at the hands of the French Nation, which kept a ragtag army of spirited colonial guerrillas under George Washington "in being," brought thirteen new nations into existence. Those nations were uneasily cobbled together in a loose confederation. The United States of America as it was governed at that time was a loose gaggle of thirteen sovereign and independent nations. As long as Britain promised the infant American Confederacy a "Round 2" war as "payback" for the Revolution, which she did, the fragile nation overlooked its internal differences, including the institution of slavery, which was disappearing in the North, and maintained its ill-defined union. As soon as the successful conclusion of the Round 2 war--the War of 1812--convinced both Americans at home and European powers overseas that the United States of America was here to stay, the septic, but bandaged-over sectional differences between the "North" and the "South" metamorphosed into an "Irrepressible Conflict" that, like a parasitic organism seeking ingress into a weakening host, sucked at the foundations of what the Sociological Imagination of the United States really was.

In 1844, in one of his earliest public speeches, Abraham Lincoln (www.goodreads.com/quotes/135212) said: "From whence shall we expect the approach of danger? Shall some trans-Atlantic military giant step the earth and crush us at a blow? Never. All the armies of Europe and Asia and Africa combined... could not by force take a drink from the Ohio River or make a track on the Blue Ridge in the trial of a thousand years. No, if destruction be our lot, we must ourselves be its author and finisher. As a nation of free men we will live forever or die by suicide." Only dis-union could ever make the United States vulnerable to an external threat, Lincoln believed, and this notion was the cornerstone of his political philosophy as much as his aversion to slavery was. Even though Lincoln himself was a racist, he believed slavery should be abolished. Failed antebellum policies, such as transporting freed Black slaves to Liberia in Africa, proved disastrous. Enslaved Voodoo-practicing tribal Africans had become enslaved Protestant Christian African Americans in the New World over time, and despite the best of myopic intentions, it was freed Black Americans who were dumped generations later onto the shores of tribal Africa, where they floundered. The Sociological Imagination of tribal Blacks had become the Sociological Imagination of oppressed Americans among those descendents of slaves who had survived the traumas of the Middle Passage experience. That realization changed slavery from a "peculiar institution" into a heinous sin in the eyes of northern abolitionists, and the "house divided" had to become "all one or all the other" in a Republican Lincoln-esque worldview to resolve it. Into this murky political world of antebellum politics, "States Rights" and "Federation" became explosive terms. Inflammatory barbs were flung at the party that seemed to be accruing power to itself at the time, while the other party felt its power ebbing. The sinner became more diabolical than the sin on the one hand, and the enfranchised hypocrite who pointed out the splinter in the eye of the other while ignoring the beam in his own eye was just as unrighteous. It was a people divided by a "good book" and a spongy constitution--a "house divided" indeed. Before returning to it, let's cut away the recorded justificatory hyperbole of this era as it has been bequeathed to us, and get down to the socio-political skeleton of this period of "American" history.

The Mississippi River provided the infant nation with a frontier that facilitated the balance of power being maintained between "Free" and "Slave" states being admitted into the Union. The Louisiana Purchase, obtained from France during the early stage of that war that would become our "Round 2," at first increased the regional power of the southern states in the Union because merchants in New Orleans controlled the economies of farmers north of the Ohio River that had to ship their produce down the nexus of rivers that flowed into the delta. Despite anti-slavery inclinations, Ohio Valley farmers would not deprive their families' bread for a lofty ideal. Neither would New York City Democrats, who earned their bread peddling northern manufactures and southern produce to European markets. This era of Southern power was reflected in the majority of the first presidents of the United States coming from the South. A northern perspective that favored a strong central government with broad powers that were constitutionally derived was trying to vie with a southern "States' Rights" view of governmental prominence that was glued together via a very circumscribed view of the Constitution. These competing ideologies came to a head in the War of 1812, when President Jefferson, a plantation-owner from Virginia, and the author of the Kentucky and Virginia Resolutions, which articulated the States' Rights point of view, enacted a Federal embargo of U.S. trade with Britain during the Napoleonic Wars as a means of discouraging British depredations on American shipping. This policy favored southern interests so much so that New England states convened the Hartford Convention to discuss secession from a pro-southern Union and make a separate peace with Great Britain, a prospect that Britain heartily endorsed. The resources of a region were threatened and the region reacted defensively, in this case, the North. The conclusion of peace before such a prospect was seriously acted on led to the second consequence of the Louisiana Purchase--westward expansion.

Westward Expansion and its "sanctified" ideal of Manifest Destiny favored both northern and southern policies "in the moment" because it vented sectional strife to an expanding frontier that both sides hoped to exploit for gaining seats, and thereby power, in Congress. In this second consequence of the Louisiana Purchase, the South was at a disadvantage. Sovereign Mexican land cramped the possibilities of southern migration. The Mexican War and the Compromises of 1820 and 1850 were all justified political expedients that temporarily diluted the simmering divisions within the nation. All were related to resources, which were founded upon "free" and/or "slave" labor. The relative barrenness of the lands geography bequeathed to the South, and the shift of economic and political power to the North in the mid-Nineteenth Century, after the opening of the Erie Canal had siphoned northern agricultural produce away form New Orleans and re-directed it to the ports of Chicago, Cleveland, Buffalo, and New York City on the Erie Canal maritime system, coupled with the increasing political pressure on slavery as Northern power deepened, caused Southerners to talk openly about secession. Southern planters would not deny their families' bread over a "peculiar institution." The resources of a region were threatened and the region reacted defensively, in this case, the South.

Much ink was spilled then, and much now, over the "right" of the Southern states to secede from the "Union." I will mention two: "States' Rights and the Union" by Forrest McDonald and "The South was Right!" by James and Walter Kennedy. To me, that "right" seemed more justifiable before the war, when legal nuances seemed pliable, than after; but I have not delved enough into the legalities of constitutional law to make a more declarative judgment. Legalists at the time failed to make a more declarative judgment as well, and in the end, much blood would be spilled to re-write the Constitution, delete the Three-fifths article, make citizens of Black Americans, and re-unite the Union according to the Northern point of view. Lawrence Kreiser and Randal Allred addressed this in their book "The Civil War in Popular Culture: Meaning and Memory" when they wrote: " The results of the Union triumph were as stupendous as the effort and cost to achieve them. The United States and its republican form of government survived--not a foregone conclusion among many domestic and foreign observers in the mid-nineteenth century. Recognizing the perpetual nature of their nation, Americans since 1865 have referred to 'the United States" rather than "these United States.'" (p 9) It was a seismic shift in political consciousness. I, personally, will not elevate one politicized point of view over another. But, I will say that the war was fought about slavery. It was fought for Union. It was fought for States' Rights. It was fought about taxes and tariffs. It was fought about votes. It was fought about power. It was fought about loyalty. It was fought about all of these, and all of these factors are ultimately subsumed under the idea that the war was fought about resources, as all wars always are. What is ironic is that most justifiers for wars claim that they are not fought over resources. To fight over resource acquisition seems crass and tacky, and is masked by noble terms such as "Manifest Destiny", "From Sea to Shining Sea", "E Pluribus Unum", "Unite or Die", "In God We Trust", etc. Alas. The Civil War ended in 1865, and it became another facet of the collective American Sociological Imagination. The rest of this essay will focus on how that Sociological Imagination became for those re-investigating, re-living, and re-enacting the war, "The Immortal Imagination."

"Perhaps no other event has captured the national imagination to the extent the Civil War has…. More books have been written about Abraham Lincoln than any other figure in world history, with the exception of Jesus Christ." (Kreiser and Randall, p.2.) That being the case, Kreiser and Randall argue that it is absolutely necessary to assess "the intersection of the Civil War and popular culture by recognizing how memories and commemorations of the war have changed since it ended in 1865." The Immortal Imagination is not only about the memory of the war itself; it is also the story of the re-imagining of the era of Reconstruction that followed the war. Frank Wetta and Martin Novelli in their book: "The Long Reconstruction: The Post-Civil War South in History, Film, and Memory" claim that "in trying to understand Reconstruction as event, as experience, and as myth, it is helpful to understand what Reconstruction meant and the issues it presented to the people who lived through it…. Beyond the immediate issues of secession and emancipation, the racial and political struggle that determined the sixteen years of the American Civil War and Reconstruction era remained in vital ways unresolved, continuing to vex the nation for generations." To Wetta and Novelli, there are three essential themes in the post-Civil War fight for the history of Reconstruction. The first was the North's attempt to re-order the political and social system of the rebel states. This approach became stillborn once an assassin's bullet extinguished Lincoln's "malice towards none" approach. The second theme was the South's reaction to the political, economic, and social consequences of the war in the wake of the maelstrom of vengeance that the Radical Republicans visited on the "conquered" South, who would pay for in resources the price of their reformation. The third, and much more organic, theme was the memory, and the contest over the memory, of the events of those sixteen years. (pp. 2-3). That amoeba is still shape-shifting.

In looking at the economic impact of the Civil War upon the South, Roger Ransom, in his article entitled "The Economics of the Civil War" concluded: "The result was an economy that remained heavily committed not only to agriculture, but to the staple crop of cotton. Crop output in the South fell dramatically at the end of the war, and had not yet recovered its antebellum level by 1879. The loss of income was particularly hard on white Southerners; per capita income of whites in 1857 had been $125; in 1879 it was just over $80…. Over the last quarter of the nineteenth century, gross crop output in the South rose by about one percent per year at a time when the GNP of United States (including the South) was rising at twice that rate. By the end of the century, Southern per capita income had fallen to roughly two-thirds the national level, and the South was locked in a cycle of poverty that lasted well into the twentieth century. How much of this failure was due solely to the war remains open to debate. What is clear is that neither the dreams of those who fought for an independent South in 1861 nor the dreams of those who hoped that a "New South" might emerge from the destruction of war after 1865 were realized." One scholar calculates the economic loss of the South at the time as two thousand million dollars. (Wetta and Novelli, p. 89.)

It would be hard to argue that the shift in the Sociological Imagination of the Reconstruction era was not heavily influenced by access to resources and the loss of resources. A psychological truth is that when one acts out anti-socially due to "troubles," one "blames the victim." Jim Crow would be sociological retribution for a resource-based contemporary "trouble." A resource-bereft South was guilty of its perpetration, and a resource-sated North was guilty of turning a blind eye in the new nation that it was re-creating "in its own image." President Andrew Johnson, Lincoln's successor, claimed he was anti-slavery, but not anti-South. In the end, he did little for the freed slave, and failed to ingratiate white Southerners. Jim Crow was based on racism, just as slavery had been justified by racism. In fact, the racist justification for the chattel enslavement of Blacks can be traced back to the "Father of Sociology," the Fourteenth Century Muslim scholar Ibn Khaldun, In his "Muqaddimah"--An Introduction to History--he dehumanizes Blacks and makes them sub-human: "the Negro nations are, as a rule, submissive to slavery, because (Negroes) have little that is (essentially) human and possess attributes that are quite similar to those of dumb animals, as we have seen." (p. 117.) What "we have seen," catalogued on preceding pages, is the "cutting-edge" socio-scientific analysis of its day: Blacks need to be man-handled because, living near the equator in searing-sunshine, their blood is more heated, and therefore their temperaments are more volatile. (pps. 53-64.) In this segment is also reiterated the justification of the biblical Hamitic curse for the perpetual enslavement of Blacks. As the lucrative machinery of sub-Saharan slave-trading became a "spoil of war" coveted by competing mercantilist nations, the racist justification for such covetousness became an intrinsic part of the sociological package. Portuguese mercantilists gobbled the trade from the Muslims, the Spanish from the Portuguese, the Dutch, French, and British mercantilists wrangled over it, with the British eventually appropriating it as booty in the Asiento agreements that ended the War of Jenkin's Ear in the middle of the Eighteenth Century. Imported racism disappeared from the Hispanic colonies like Brazil when slavery was abolished at the end of the Nineteenth Century because the three million slaves established there vastly outnumbered the few Iberian colonials, and miscegenation with native populations bred racism from the social landscape and the resources of the new nation were not parsed out according to racial ideology, except for the marginalized indigenous peoples of the Amazon basin. Not so in the United States, where the quarter million imported slaves, even though they had bred to four million by 1860, were still a distinctive minority in a Caucasian population, and racism justified their disenfranchisement from resources. After the Civil War, the racism that was imported into the colonies with the slaves, grew more rabid in the immediate antebellum years and became more exacerbated in the Reconstruction era by Southern whites, who now felt themselves threatened by Black access to resources, as well as Northern Whites, who were happy to see slaves emancipated, but resisted with vehement racist notions of their own, Black migration to the industrial centers of the North, where they would be competitors for wages. In later years, the Cold War mantra of anti-imperialism chanted by the Eisenhower administration to the imperial powers in Africa to de-colonize prompted a bewildered Black population in the United States, suffering under Jim Crow, to organize and rally during the Civil Rights Era of the 1950's and 60's. The iconoclastic traumas of 1968 turned suit-and-tie lower middle-class Blacks seeking enfranchisement into militant Black Power radicals that were fed up with dollops and sops of power. "We shall overcome" became "Ain't no stoppin' us now," and racism became a tool in the kit of Black activists like Leonard Jeffries who, in the 1990's, turned Ibn Khaldun on his head by claiming that Black people, as "Sun People," were tranquil and pacific, while the "Ice People," those whose genetics were honed in the climate of the Ice Age-- Caucasians and Jews--were "cold-hearted" and, by nature, were intrinsically violent and cruel. What did Johnson's "Great Society" engender? How has it played out in the Sociological Imagination of the United States today? It depends on whom you ask. The rhetoric of race as a social construct really masks the fundamental human primal drive for resources--that "tacky" explanation again. It is tragic-comical how humans dress the drive for resources with myopic cultural and sub-cultural mythologies. That is a main theme in this essay as one can tell. It is in trying to tear through the veil of divisive rhetoric that rends us as a people, and encourage us to re-examine the constitutional basis of what an "American" really is that has motivated me, admittedly in part, to write this book.

According to the African American historian W.E.B. DuBois, the Reconstruction era, from 1861-1890, was the "onset of the Age of Segregation and Disenfranchisement." (Wetta and Novelli, p. 2.) The Sociological Imagination can travel along many paths. In the sociological "memory" of the South, the Reconstruction era is the period when the myth of the "Lost Cause" was spawned. Let us look at that now.

Historian James Horton has been quoted as claiming that 80% of Americans receive no formal training in history beyond high school. (Robert Weir in Kreiser and Allred. p. 62.) Historical tourism in the form of museum visiting, battlefield touring, Living History immersing, and historical re-enacting "shape what is remembered." After secondary school, much historical information, often agenda-driven, reaches the "historical" ears of the bulk of Americans via Living History activities and historical re-enactments. This is deliberate. Weir argues (p. 62.) that the creature that was "Abraham Lincoln" has morphed chameleon-like in the American Imagination in the seven score and ten years since his death. He remembers that Lincoln's point in prosecuting the Civil War in the Gettysburg Address was the hallowness of "an unfinished work" that portended "a new birth of freedom" at that war's conclusion. Weir follows this with an excerpt from Lincoln's Second Inaugural Address: "one-eighth of the whole population were colored slaves, not distributed generally over the Union, but localized in the southern part of it. These slaves constituted a peculiar and powerful interest. All knew that this interest was somehow the cause of the war."

After Reconstruction, emancipation quickly gave way to reconciliation. The northern agenda of reconstituting the South in its own image was bearing fruit. The hydraulic power inherent in the piedmont region of the Carolinas and Georgia were harnessed to industrialize the South and integrate its economy into the economic machinery of the Northern mercantile system. Greensboro--Winston-Salem, Charlotte-Concord, and Greenville-Spartanburg blossomed, while Atlanta rose like a phoenix from the ashes. At the same time, Europe was fully committed to its spate of industrial competition, and that is what spurred the Age of Imperialism in Africa and Asia. The new "all-steel" navies, which made Britain's armada of "wooden walls" obsolete virtually overnight, soon glutted the Atlantic, the Mediterranean, and the Pacific with dreadnaughts. Japan, awakened from its medieval Tokugawa torpor, soon joined the feeding frenzy. The resources of these regions were threatened and they reacted defensively, by recklessly thrusting outwardly. In 1883, British Empire commentator Sir John Seeley remarked laconically: "we seem, as it were, to have conquered and peopled half the world in a fit of absence of mind." (www.britishempire.co.uk/article/evangelicalempire.htm) And the United States after 1865, in its turn, was poised to flex its imperial muscle in the Caribbean and the Pacific to both expand and protect its shores and its trade. It was the time when Rudyard Kipling wrote "The White Man's Burden" to mentor his Anglo-Saxon brethren in the United States to: "take up the White Man's burden; send forth the best ye breed. Go bind your sons to exile, to serve your captives' need; to wait in heavy harness, on fluttered folk and wild--your new-caught, sullen peoples, half-devil and half-child."

Simultaneously with the burgeoning of the "fin-de-siècle" era in Europe--a time of millenarian dread and aesthetic escapism--the "Lost Cause" gained momentum in the Immortal Imagination of the South; and the North, as an indulgent brother, nodded in acquiescence. Memorials at Civil War battlefields downplayed the sectional wounds that were still so raw and offered somber testimonials to the dead. By the 1890's, the Civil War was transformed from a war among the States to a conflict among "brothers" in the popular imagination. American imperialism bound white Americans together. In 1913, at the 50th Anniversary commemoration of the Battle of Gettysburg, President Woodrow Wilson opened his July 4th speech to a crowd that included over 50,000 Civil War veterans, with the words: " I need not tell you what the Battle of Gettysburg meant…. " It brought "peace and unity and vigor, and the maturity and might of a great nation. We have found one another again as brothers and comrades…. Enemies no longer… our battles long past, the quarrel forgotten." (p. 66.) 1913 also marked the breaking point of the angst-ridden skein of tensions that hallmarked "fin-de-siècle" Europe. By the summer of the next year, the "powder keg" would explode. In 1917, the year the United States entered World War I, "Virginia became the first former Confederate state to erect a memorial at Gettysburg--a battle scene topped by Robert E. Lee astride a horse." The governor of Virginia opened the dedication by assuring: "We are not here to consider the reasons for this conflict.'" The keynote speaker, Leigh Robinson, soon followed and dubbed the southern cause "sacred." "We assemble to commemorate catastrophe."… Virginia would have abolished slavery in the 1840's, "but for the intemperance of northern fanatics." He even asserted that "slavery had been a positive experience and declared that the slave trade was evil, not bondage itself. 'The South did not desert the Union;… the Union deserted the South.'" (pp. 66-7.) To finish a thought; after World War I, the "Scramble for Africa" would devolve into a futile and dishonorable miasma, upon which President Eisenhower would later exert pressure in order to stoke the engine of "de-colonization" that would take the steam out of the Soviet Union's charges of "First World" hypocrisy before a "Third World" audience. De-colonization was more about politics, which were all about resources than it was about people. Ironically, Kruschev's "We will bury you!" prophecy was also more about resource productivity under a socialist ideology than a trumpet call for communal humanitarianism under a red banner. But, that should not be surprising. Alas.

What is the "Lost Cause?" In his article "Oh, I'm a Good Ol' Rebel," Christopher Bates, in the Kreiser and Allred book, wrote: "The bedrock of the Lost Cause was romantic imagery--gentlemanly Robert E. Lee, daring Stonewall Jackson, magnolias and cotton fields, the idyllic life of the plantations. These appealing notions were the anchor for a series of ideas about the war--that the Confederacy never really had a chance of winning, but almost did anyway, that the South's purpose was to fight not for slavery but for states' rights and so forth. The purpose of the Lost Cause was twofold: to redeem the tarnished image of the South and make a case to northerners for the southern states' full reinstatement into the Union (under white leadership), and to help the defeated Confederates come to grips with their loss of the war." (p. 196.) Bates' definition is pure Sociological Imagination "troubles" in the pure strain of Mills. In this vein, it is unsurprising that the bittersweet memory of sacrifice at the Battle of Gettysburg epitomizes the memory of the Lost Cause more than the greatest victory of the Confederacy at the Battle of Chancellorsville, fought two months earlier.

In his book "American History Through the Hollywood Film," Melvyn Stokes has written: "The last few years have seen a dramatic growth in the use of Hollywood feature films dealing with American history in college and school classrooms on both sides of the Atlantic. In an increasing image-conscious and image-oriented culture, students often engage deeply with such films and discuss with enthusiasm the interpretations they offer of the past." (p. 1.) D.W. Griffith, as early as the first decade of the Twentieth century, had recognized this: the movie camera "was the instrument with which history was beginning to be written. The truths of history today are restricted to the limited few attending our colleges and universities; the motion picture can carry these truths to the entire world,... while at the same time bringing diversion to the masses." Renowned for the brilliant cinematic techniques it introduced, Griffith's "Birth of a Nation," though denied, was a recruiting tool for the KKK, and it showcased the Lost Cause on celluloid. Stokes goes on to say: Most Americans' view of the Civil War and Reconstruction period is still profoundly shaped by "Gone with the Wind".... Ninety percent of today's U.S. population is believed to have seen the movie at least once.... Both films are idols erected to the "best" sentiments of the Lost Cause and through necessity depict slavery, but as a benign and paternal institution coddling happy and nurtured sambos." (p. 3.)

After the Civil Rights era and the militant turn of the Black Power movement, "race" and "racism" climbed to the summit of the pedestal of the American Sociological Imagination as the root cause of the Civil War. "Roots" was released in 1977, and in 1997, Steven Spielberg released his film "Amistad" to highlight this. He nailed his understanding of the amorphous nature of this imagination when, at a 2012 Dedication Day speech at Gettysburg, he said: "Through art we bring what is lost back to us, to bring the dead back to life. This resurrection is, of course, just an illusion, it's a fantasy and it's a dream, but dreams matter somehow to us." Amistad was Spielberg's homage to a northern "Lost Cause" vision. Ironically, the graphic images of slavery it depicted pleased no one. Whites reacted negatively to the Middle Passage scenes, and Blacks found them degrading and masochistic. (pp. 5-6.) Robert Burgoyne in his article "Race and Nation in Glory" in Robert Eberwein's "The War Film," calls the film "Glory" a re-mythologized work of both history, folklore, and zeitgeist. It is a subtle and complex film inculcating "the contemporary map of liberal thinking" and is intended to "reshape the identity of race and nation." A mystical sense of nationhood is forged in the maturation process of idealistic youth being tempered in the crucible of battle. In the end, the de-humanized slave and the pampered abolitionist are buried together in 1862 in a hecatomb of heroes that will act as a "chrysalis" of injecting racial identity into the national identity more than 100 years later. (pp. 65-70.)

The Sociological Imagination concerning the issue of slavery was, and always will be, the hub around which worldviews about the Civil War will revolve. Gary Gallagher, in his Great Courses lectures on the American Civil War, documented that race and racism merged with the northern notions of mercantilism in the platforms of the Republican Party in the 1856 and 1860 presidential campaigns to counter the race and racism notions of the "old constitutional" platforms of the agrarian south. In the midst of the heady days of secession, Alexander Stevens said: "Our new government is founded upon the great truth that the Negro is not equal to the White Man, that slavery is his natural and moral condition. This, our new government, is the first in the history of the world based upon this great physical, philosophical, and moral truth." Jefferson Davis, in a message to the Confederate Congress in late April 1861, said: "The labor of African slaves was, and is, indispensible to the South's economic development. With interests of such overwhelming magnitude imperiled, the people of the southern states were driven by the conduct of the North to the adoption of some course of action to avert the danger to which they were openly menaced." (cd 16--The Background to Emancipation.) The former statement concerns racism, the latter, resources. By 1861, the two were intimately linked in extremis. At the other extreme, by 2007, the Black Power movement had yielded a book by Leone Bennett Jr. entitled "Forced into Glory" that turned the Abraham Lincoln "myth" on its head. It purports that Lincoln was nothing but a wily politician and a white supremacist racist from his birth until his death, and that his "pseudo-abolitionism" was merely a political ploy to re-unite the Union. Solicitude for a people in bondage was not part of the equation.

"North Carolina's role in the Civil War is fraught with contradictions.... Any volume that attempts to recount the Civil War in North Carolina must come to grips with these and other contradictions--real or imagined." So say authors Buck Yearns and John Barrett in their book "North Carolina Civil War Documentary." (p. xi.) There were die-hard secessionists in 1860. A March 4, 1861 article in the Wilmington Journal stated their case: "Mr. Davis re-stated and summed this up, by emphatically declaring that the South could never--never obtain any better or more satisfactory terms while she remained in the present Union, and for his part he could never assent to the terms contained in this report of the Peace Congress, as in accordance with the honor or the interests of the South. Never!"

"Everything showed the spirit of the Republicans. They had passed the most oppressive tariff that had ever been heard of. They would tax us to death to protect and build up themselves, and at the same time pay the agents of the underground Railroad for running off our negroes. How could Wilmington, oppressed by a tariff of forty per cent and upwards, expect to hold her own with Georgetown or Charleston, or any port of the Confederate States, with ten per cent duties?"

"No arrangement had been made--none would be made. The division must be made on the line of slavery. The South must go with the South, and not with any new-fangled central Republic, or as the tail-end and victim of a Free Soil North…." (pp. 21-2.)

In North Carolina, there were also those called "middle-of-the-roaders," who were caught between the Union and secession: "A Confederacy or Union composed of the fifteen slaveholding states would, after a while, encounter some of the same difficulties which now beset the existing Union. The States south of us would produce and export cotton, while the middle or bread-stuff States would become deeply interested in manufactures. Foreigners from Europe and the North would pour into the latter, and push the slave population farther south. Manufacturers would demand and obtain protection, and free labor would contend with and root out slave labor in the middle States, until at length the latter would commence to agitate against the cotton States as the North is now agitating against us," with the possibility of the Confederacy splitting up into two new Confederacies.

"The two Confederacies… would meet as rivals at foreign courts and in foreign markets. Their ministers and merchants would partake of the spirit of the people at home, and they would cripple each other and involve themselves in endless and most injurious complications in their intercourse with foreign powers." (p. 8.)

There were also pro-Unionists. Even months after secession, William Littlejohn, a prominent lawyer from Washington County, wrote to the governor: "Lincoln has done nothing wrong, nothing unconstitutional, nothing but what his oath of office constrained him to do." (p. 27.)

In the end, North Carolina became the last non-border Southern state to secede from the Union, on May 20, 1861. She claimed that she was "coerced" into secession and war when Abraham Lincoln chose to raise 75,000 volunteer troops and put down armed insurrection in South Carolina after Fort Sumter was fired on and reduced to rubble in the harbor of Charleston, South Carolina in early 1861. To subdue South Carolina, Federal troops would have to "invade" North Carolina. This would happen. In "the War of Northern Aggression," 125,000 North Carolinians would serve under Confederate colors and 1/3rd of them would die, the worst casualty rate of any state in the Confederacy. North Carolina had 1/9th the population of the Confederacy, but provided 1/6th-1/7th of the Confederacy's solders; she also had the most deserters. North Carolina was a secondary theater during the war, but was a strategic center for the Confederate war effort. Blockaded by the Union navy almost from the outset, North Carolina provided massive resources for the Army of Northern Virginia in terms of men, material, and foodstuffs. During the war, most of her coastline was abandoned to Federal troops due to insufficient manpower resources in the "home" state, and North Carolina often felt she was being "sacrificed by the high command for the defense of Virginia." The Danville railroad connection was virtually the only logistical artery that supplied Richmond, and providing Virginia's sustenance proved "injurious to North Carolina's best interests." Governor Zebulon Vance, North Carolina's strong States' Rights advocate, at one time threatened to use North Carolina state militia to shoot any Confederate troops who continued to impress foodstuffs from her soil. He was often at wits end trying to maintain the sovereignty of his state while supporting the Southern cause.

In the welter of the early days of the armed conflict remembered as the Civil War, the 22nd North Carolina Infantry Regiment was raised. The following history of the regiment is culled directly from the webpage of the modern re-enactor's unit:

"The 22nd Regiment of North Carolina Troops was organized in camp near Raleigh in July, 1861, by the election of the following field officers: Colonel J. Johnston Pettigrew, of Tyrrell county, then a resident of Charleston, S. C. Colonel Pettigrew had seen service with the forces in South Carolina, and commanded a regiment at the siege and capture of Fort Sumter by the Confederates in April, 1861."

"Until March 2, 1862, the regiment remained in support of the batteries at Evansport, in brigade at different times with the 1st Arkansas, the 2nd Tennessee, a Virginia regiment, and perhaps other regiments, under command, in the order named, of Generals John G. Walker, Isaac R. Trimble, and Samuel G. French. While there the health of the men was good, except for measles, which seemed to be epidemic in all the regiments. The batteries were frequently engaged with the enemy's gunboats, and with batteries on the Maryland side of the Potomac, but the casualties were very few. Company I had several men wounded by the bursting of a forty-two-pounder gun in Battery No. 2. While on duty at Evansport, Colonel Pettigrew was promoted brigadier-general, but feeling that his services were of more value in furthering the re-enlistment and re-organization of the regiment, then near at hand, he declined the appointment--a rare instance of patriotism and devotion to the public good. When the army fell back from Manassas and the Potomac in March, 1862, to the line of the Rappahannock, General French commanded the brigade which took post at Fredericksburg. Soon after General French was transferred to a command in North Carolina, and the regiment was marched to the peninsula below Richmond and shared in the Williamsburg and Yorktown campaign. Returning to the vicinity of Richmond, and Colonel Pettigrew having been again appointed brigadier, in command of the brigade, which appointment he this time accepted, Lieutenant-Colonel Charles E. Lightfoot, previously of the 6th Regiment, was promoted colonel. Under his command the regiment went into the fight at Seven Pines in May-June, 1862, in which it was heavily engaged and its losses were severe. General Pettigrew was here wounded and made prisoner. Colonel Lightfoot was also captured. Captain Thomas D. Jones and Lieutenant S. H. Adams were killed, besides many others, and the aggregate loss of the regiment was 147 in all."

"Soon after Seven Pines the regiment was re-organized, when the following were elected field officers: James Connor, of South Carolina, colonel; Captain Robert H. Gray, of Company L, lieutenant-colonel, and Captain Columbus C. Cole, of Company E, major. They took rank from June 14th, 1862. There were many changes also in the line officers. Previously Adjutant Graham Dares had been promoted captain and assigned to duty as assistant adjutant-general on the general staff, and Lieutenant P. E. Charles became adjutant. A new brigade, too, was formed, consisting of the 16th, 22nd, 34th, and 38th North Carolina Regiments, and placed under the command of Brigadier-General Wm. D. Pender, in the division of General A. P. Hill."

"An officer in describing the bearing of the 22nd at Seven Pines, says: "In all my readings of veterans, and of coolness under fire, I have never conceived of anything surpassing the coolness of our men in this fight.""

"In the "Seven Days' Fight" around Richmond the regiment was next engaged: First, at Mechanicsville, June 26th, in which Colonel Connor was badly wounded; at Ellison's Mill; at Gaines' Mill, June 27th, where it won the highest encomiums. General A. P. Hill says of it in his report of the battle: "The 16th North Carolina, Colonel McElroy, and the 22nd, Lieutenant-Colonel Gray, at one time carried the crest of the hill, and were in the enemy's camp, but were driven back by overwhelming numbers." And General Pender: "My men fought nobly and maintained their ground with great stubbornness." Next at Frazier's Farm, June 30th. In this fight the regiment was very conspicuous and suffered severely. Among the killed were Captain Harper and Lieutenant P. E. Charles, of Company E. The latter was bearing the regimental colors at the time, and near him, in a space little more than ten feet square, nine men of the color guard lay dead. Captain Ephraim Bouldin, of Company H, was also killed."

"On August 9th the battle of Cedar Mountain was fought. In this engagement the 22nd Regiment was charged by a regiment of cavalry which it easily repulsed and punished sharply. Lieutenant Robert W. Cole, of Company E, succeeded Lieutenant Charles as adjutant. The regiment was with Jackson in his battles with Pope of August 28th and 29th, and bore an active part at Second Manassas on August 30th. In these actions it was efficiently commanded by Major C. C. Cole, owing to the extreme sickness of Lieutenant-Colonel Gray. Two days later it was again engaged with the enemy at Chantilly, or Ox Hill, fought in a terrible thunder storm, in which the artillery of heaven and of earth seemed to strive in rivalry. The hard service and heavy losses of this campaign may be understood by the fact that at this time there were, out of the twelve field officers of the four regiments of the brigade, but three left on duty with their commands, and some of the companies were commanded by corporals."

"Pope, the braggart, had made good use of his "Headquarters in the Saddle" to get out of Virginia, and had learned all about "Lines of Retreat.""

"The 22nd Regiment took part in the reduction and capture of Harper's Ferry on August 15th, where it remained until the 17th, the day the battle of Sharpsburg was fought. On that day the regiment, with the rest of A. P. Hill's Division, arrived on the battle-field after a forced march of seventeen miles, in time to aid in the afternoon in the decided repulse of Burnside's attack at the "Stone Bridge," thereby preventing the turning of General Lee's right and saving the day to the Confederates. On the night of the 18th the army recrossed the Potomac, and on the 19th was followed by a division of Federals, which was promptly attacked by a part of A. P. Hill's command, routed and driven back across the Potomac at Shepherdstown with great slaughter. The 22nd took an active part in this successful fight. After the enemy had been driven into the river, a heavy fire was opened on the Confederates by the Federal batteries and sharpshooters from its northern bank. Under this fire a detachment of the 22nd, under Major Cole, lay, with very slight protection, for nearly twelve hours, and could be withdrawn only after nightfall."

"Shortly after Shepherdstown, Lieutenant-Colonel Gray rejoined the regiment, and Lieutenant J. R. Cole, previously of the 54th Regiment, was assigned to the 22nd as adjutant. On November 22, A. P. Hill's Division, which had been on duty near Martinsburg and at Snicker's Gap in the Blue Ridge (where there was constant skirmishing), marched for Fredericksburg, where it arrived on the 2nd of December, a distance of 180 miles. In this winter march many of the men were barefooted, but made merry over it. At the Battle of Fredericksburg, December 13, Jackson's Corps formed the right of Lee's army, and Pender's Brigade was on the left of A. P. Hill's Division in the first line. The regiment acquitted itself in this famous action in a way well worthy its old reputation. The night of the 12th a detail from the regiment by a bold dash succeeded in burning a number of haystacks and houses very near to, and affording cover to, the Federal lines. Major C. C. Cole was in charge of the detail, and next day commanded the skirmish line in front of Pender's Brigade. He was ably seconded by Captain Laban Odell, of Company M., and Lieutenant Clark, of Company A. The brigade maintained its position throughout the action, repulsing every attack upon it, but not without heavy loss. Major Cole was much complimented for his handsome action in dispersing the strong force of the enemy's skirmishers on the brigade front. General Pender was wounded, and his aide-de-camp, Lieutenant Sheppard, was killed in the engagement. Some time before Fredericksburg the 13th North Carolina Regiment, Colonel Alfred M. Scales, had been added to Pender's Brigade. The winter of 1862-'3 was passed in picket and other duty on the Rappahannock below Fredericksburg. Colonel James Conner rejoined the regiment while it was stationed there, but was still unfitted by his severe wound for active duty. The services of Lieutenant-Colonel Gray were lost to the regiment at this time. Always a man of delicate health, he died 16th of March, 1863. Major C. C. Cole was promoted to lieutenant-colonel and Captain Odell became major, their commissions dating March 16, 1862--positions that these excellent officers were to hold but a short time.
At Chancellorsville in May, 1863, the regiment was in Jackson's flank attack on Hooker, and throughout the whole of the action was heavily engaged. Its losses were very severe. Colonel Cole and Major Odell were both killed, 219 men and twenty-six out of thirty-three officers were killed or wounded, and though the regiment was distinguished by its accustomed efficiency and gallantry, nothing could compensate for the terrible destruction. Chancellorsville was the eighteenth battle of the 22nd Regiment, and the most fatal. It went through the Maryland campaign of 1863 and Gettysburg with credit. General Wm. D. Pender had been made a major-general and was now in command of the division, and Colonel Alfred M. Scales, of the 13th Regiment, was promoted brigadier in command of the brigade. It participated in the first day's brilliant success at Gettysburg, was engaged also on the second day, and on the third the brigade was part of General I. R. Trimble's Division, General Pender having been mortally wounded in support of Heth's Division, then under Pettigrew, in the famous charge on Cemetery Heights. In this charge, Archer's and Scales' Brigades occupied and held for a time the Federal works, and when they retreated to the Confederate lines, Scales' Brigade had not one field officer left for duty, and but very few line officers. Its total loss was 102 killed and 322 wounded."

I stop with Gettysburg because it is the 150th Anniversary of that battle that prompted the writing of this book. I will also return to the topic of media once again. Newspapers and documented speeches have been already utilized in this essay, but the new medium of photography soon added its own sociological "McLuhan-esque" message to the Immortal Imagination of the Civil War. This has been studied by Jeff Rosenheim in his book: Photography and the American Civil War." I will leave it to Keith to flesh out the medium of photography in the Civil War at the time and in his modern recapitulation of its technology, but I will highlight those points that are germane to the Immortal Imagination of the Civil War in the American Sociological Imagination. Daguerrotypes, invented by Jacques Daguerre in the early Nineteenth Century, reached numbers of 25 million in the 1840's and 1850's. Matthew Brady had opened his own daguerrotype studio in 1844 in New York City. He photographed celebrities such as John C. Calhoun, Daniel Webster, John James Audobon, and "curiosities," such as P.T. Barnum's "Tom Thumb." Daguerrotypes were reproducible from glass to paper, but were expensive to produce; hence only the wealthy could sit for their time-consuming "imperial" portraits. Much attention, therefore, was given to props and poses. War portraiture would include Abraham Lincoln, Jefferson Davis, George McLellan, and Robert E. Lee. The common soldier too was drawn to portraiture, but in lieu of the expensive daguerrotypes that were beyond his means, the cheap, but non-reproducible tintype, was affordable to him. In the days before "dog tags," these "imperial" portraits reproduced the stiff, dour images that have come down to us because the subject could not move during the lengthy time of photographic exposure. In the event of death in wartime, these photographs could help in identifying decayed corpses and notifying the next of kin. They also could be shipped back home as final mementos of their fallen loved ones. (pp. 17-23.) It is in this vein that Keith photographed members of the 22nd North Carolina Infantry Regiment and which are reproduced in the pages that follow.

It is necessary to link the 22nd North Carolina Infantry Regiment with its modern, re-enactor brethren, and put re-enacting into its proper sociological construct. There have been some unintended consequences that have accrued to the notion of the "Lost Cause." Christopher Bates, cited before, has written that "because actual backward-looking racists--the Ku Klux Klan, the League of the South, Dixie Republic, some neo-Nazi groups--have made extensive use of the Confederacy and its symbols, particularly the Confederate battle flag and the common soldier of the Confederate army. The South in general, and any person who utilizes or affiliates with these symbols in particular, has suffered by association." Living History re-enactors are obvious targets; the NAACP has condemned re-enacting as a manifestation of "Southern racism" and called for the abolition of Confederate re-enacting altogether. Re-enactors counter that 200,000 Black soldiers fought for the Confederacy, and African Americans today re-enact in Civil War re-enactments in Confederate units and march under the "Stars and Bars." Today also, "Lost Cause" stereotypes adhere to Southerners, in general: "Southerners are fine people, but they're a little behind the times. I think they're kinda slow. They're fine, if they'd only stop fighting the Civil War. They're lazy, shiftless and ignorant. They carry their racial prejudice too far." And "Lost Cause" stereotypes follow re-enactors, in particular. They are outcasts, drunks, and Rednecks.

Studies show that Civil War re-enactors are generally white, older, and conservative. Of the northerners, westerners, southerners, foreigners--there are many Civil War re-enactor groups in Europe and Australia--and African Americans-- there are even Native American Civil War re-enactors, 2/3 of them want to be Confederates. This reveals the "Walter Mitty" element of re-enacting. Modern, industrial automatons, punching time clocks and hoping to live long enough to collect Social Security, would rather sport a feather in their hats and grow unkempt beards while yipping the "Rebel Yell" in a weekend re-enactment than shave, wear the monotonous blue uniform of the Federals, and shout the Yankee "Huzzah" in a re-enactment. Many Southerners join a re-enactment unit in order to honor their ancestors and their heritage. Many Northerners, who fight in Confederate units, also want to honor the "sacrificial" and "honorable" memories that a "Lost Cause" worldview inculcates among the units notable for that. Others are simply bored, and want to get-away-from-it-all for a while and feel a shock of adrenaline surge through their veins. Re-enacting is not for the weak-of-pocket. It is an expensive hobby. Several thousands of dollars must be invested by a die-hard re-enactor to be accoutered head-to-toe in authentic replicas--no oxymoron intended--of Civil War era uniforms and equipment, unlike the "farby," which I was, who shows up occasionally and marches into battle sporting union-benefit eyeglasses, one-size-fits-all Walmart socks, and Dr. Scholl's supported footwear. Worst of all, he borrows authentic equipment from the die-hards, who "endearingly" quip among themselves: 'He's a farby. Bless his heart.' The indolent and indigent stereotype of a Civil War re-enactor is simply false. The average northern Civil War re-enactor earned $64,000 in 2013, while the average Southern re-enactor earned $62,000. Perhaps the final point about re-enacting, and Living History, should be made by Christy Coleman. She is an African American historian and director of the American Civil War Center at the Tredegar Iron Works in Richmond, Virginia. "When it comes to the Confederate, the Confederate heritage person,...

you will often see, especially if you drive, the further south you drive, little bumper stickers that say 'Heritage, not Hate.' For those individuals that's exactly what it is, they're just honoring what their ancestors thought was right. And for me, as an African-American woman who grew up in Virginia hearing all of this foolishness, to me it is okay, I'm willing to acknowledge that, but please don't dismiss the role and the function of our folks." (pp. 193-210.)

In the interviews that follow, one will hear most of the points made in this essay stated by re-enactors of the 22nd North Carolina Infantry Regiment. I have edited their comments as little as possible in order to give genuine voice to their opinions. Minimal re-ordering was done for continuity of narrative and to fit each interview, which lasted from 10 to 30 minutes, onto a single page of text. Transcripts of every interview in the original have been preserved. Reproduced below is the questionnaire that each man or woman interviewed filled out in order to obtain permission for publication, gain standard biographical data, and prepare each person for his or her interview. The biographies of the men from the Civil War era 22nd North Carolina were obtained from Louis Manarin's "North Carolina Troops-1861-1865: A Roster."

"These" United States are now "the" United States, and the United States still needs to apply balm to its scars, some of which are still quite raw, across the board. It is hoped that this book will be found in some way medicinal. It is intended that whatever prompted then, and still prompts today, the men and women who enliven the memory of the Civil War in the United States to all have a voice in the Immortal Imagination of the Civil War, a watershed of conflict, sacrifice, and change that shaped this nation's sense of self, should be heard.

John Sheehan

REFERENCES

American Civil War reenactment. Retrieved May 13, 2015. www.en.wikipedia.org/wiki/American_Civil_War_reenactment

Bennett, L. (2007) *Forced into Glory.* Johnson Publishing Company.

Carr, R. *The Evangelical Empire: Christianity's Contribution to Victorian Colonial Expansion.* Retrieved May 13, 2015. (www.britishempire.co.uk/article/evangelicalempire.htm)

Eberwein, R. (2005) *The War Film.* New Brunswick, NJ: Rutgers University Press.

Gallagher, G. (2000) *The Great Courses: The American Civil War.* Chantilly, VA: The Teaching Company.

Ibn Khaldun. (1989) *The Muqaddimah.* Princeton, NJ: Bollingen Series.

Kennedy, J. and W. (1995) *The South was Right!* Gretna, La.: Pelican Pub. Co.

Kreiser, A. and R. Allred. (2014) *The Civil War in Popular Culture.* Lexington, Kentucky: The University Press of Kentucky.

Living History. Retrieved May 13, 2015. (www.en.wikipedia.org/wiki/Living_history)

Manarin, L. (1979) *North Carolina Troops-1861-1865: A Roster.* Raleigh, North Carolina: Division of Archives and History.

McDonald, F. (2000) *States' Rights and the Union.* Lawrence, Kansas: The University of Kansas Press.

Ransom, R. *The Economics of the Civil War.* Retrieved May 13, 2015. (eh.net/encyclopedia/the-economics-of-the-civil-war)

Rosenheim, J. (2013) *Photography and the American Civil War.* New York: Metropolitan Museum of Art.

The Sociological Imagination. Retrieved May 13, 2015. (legacy.lclark.edu/~goldman/socioimagination)

Stokes, M. (2013) *Hollywood and the American Historical Film.* NY: Bloomsbury.

Twenty Second North Carolina Infantry Regiment. Retrieved May 13, 2015. (www.22ndnorthcarolina.org/about-us/history)

Wetta, R. and M. Novelli. (2014) *The Long Reconstruction.* New York: Routledge

Yearns, B. and G. Barrett. (2002) *North Carolina Civil War Documentary.* Chapel Hill, NC: University of North Carolina Press.

Gettysburg 150th Anniversary Re-enactment Questionnaire

John Sheehan and Keith Millman are interviewing for short biographies and taking authentic tintype photographs of re-enactors of the 22nd N. Carolina regiment at the 150th Anniversary re-enactment at Gettysburg. They propose to produce a reasonably priced book of this regiment for this event, entitled The Immortal Imagination, as well as provide a free photo to each of the participants interviewed and photographed.

Name:
Date:
Phone:
Address:
Email:
Age:
Occupation:

Questions:

Where do you live?

Did you ever live in North Carolina?

Do you know the history of the 1862/3 22nd North Carolina?

Do you know the general/specific stories of any of the men in the 1862/3 22nd N. Carolina?

Do you personally re-enact any of these men?

How long have you been a re-enactor?

Why are you a re-enactor?

Do you think re-enactments serve a purpose? What is the purpose?

What do you get most out of re-enacting?

How do you connect personally with the Twenty-first Century regiment and the men?

PHOTOGRAPHER AND ASSISTANT, KEITH MILLMAN & MATHEA MILLMAN

THE VENERABLE TINTYPE

The photographs in this book were created using the same wet plate technology as photographs made during the Civil War. In the 1860s photography was a cumbersome process made by itinerant craftsmen or employees from one of the major photo studios in the larger cities. Hundreds of itinerant photographers carried cameras, chemicals, plates and a portable darkroom on wagons and stayed at the margins of the conflicts, safely visiting camps and battlefields when there was little danger.

The pictures included here, in the same way, were safely made, away from the sounds of artillery shells and the smell of gun powder in the camp of the 22nd North Carolina regiment. Two rows of white canvas tents faced each other creating a thoroughfare for the daily activities and preparation for battle for the men and defined the boundary of the regiment. Set up in a farmers field, the regiment was part of a larger encampment of the Longstreet division, surrounded by thousands of men, women and tents spread throughout the forests and fields preparing to re-enact the battle of Gettysburg in the heat and humidity of early July.

The photographer's tent was at the far end of the row of soldier's tents and here is where the portable darkroom was set up along with the large box camera, chemicals, trays and jugs of water. Over the course of three days Mathea and I photographed the men and women of the camp under the awning of the photographer's tent or in front of the modest canvas tents of the soldiers.

Portrait photography requires a complicit relationship between the photographer and the sitter. The photographer bears witness to the sitter and the sitter re-enacts himself in front of the camera. But the process is more complicated when the person posing is presenting themselves and is also posing as a soldier who served 150 years ago. For the men of the 22nd North Carolina the act of being photographed was a way of giving praise; being photographed acknowledged their historical counterpart through the authenticity of their appearance and paid homage to their comrades from another time who once stood on similar ground in southern Pennsylvania 150 years ago.

Photographing a re-enactor is extending the portrait of the soldier who originally fought on the confederate side during the civil war at Gettysburg. Each portrait captures the look of the re-enactor from the 21st century based on the original soldier from the 19th century. Each photograph contains a complex overlay of contemporary nostalgia, veneration and spectacle. Living history is an approximation needing soldiers from both time periods.

The memorializing act of photography bestows importance and commemorates the occasion of the 150 year anniversary of the battle of Gettysburg, but in addition, the photographs function by bringing two men together - the re-enactor and an original soldier bound together in the surface of the wet plate photograph.

The portraits were made efficiently; men were arranged by Mathea or posed themselves while plates were coated with light sensitive silver, loaded wet into a plate holder in the portable dark tent then placed into the back of the camera. Exposures were between 3 – 5 seconds in the hazy sun. Once exposed, plates were developed and washed. Commonly referred to as tintypes or ferrotypes these pictures were relatively cheap to make in the 1860s. They were one of a kind, durable and made on metal. The process was less than 10 years old by the time the Civil War broke out: fast, direct and portable, they became very popular at that time.

Wet Collodion emulsion is colorblind, it is more sensitive to the blue spectrum of light than red therefore blue registers lighter and warmer tones are darker on prints. This, in part, determines the tonal quality of the tintypes. The quality of the light is important as well, the light that lit the subjects in Gettysburg was the same, moderated by the heat and water in the air as it was 150 years ago; the weather is part of the pictures and most shots are in open shade, avoiding direct sun for the pictures.

Many of the photographs included here suffer from imperfections brought about by the inexperience of the photographer and the difficulty of shooting in the field. The portable dark tent was provisional. It was a temporary darkroom in a suitcase, a claustrophobic space in which to work in the dark where fumes collected in the heat and humidity of the Pennsylvania summer.

Tintypes are fragile objects prone to problems when the emulsion is soft and wet. The black metal base shows where the emulsion separated and wore off during the development and handling. The emulsion is the thinnest of films that contains the portraits of the soldiers as fragile and susceptible to damage as skin in war time. For the men who fought in the civil war, many suffered from injuries and amputations, often the subject of photography at that time, but for the re-enactors of the 22nd North Carolina, where no bullets were used, canon shells were not live and combatants were not allowed to engage each other, there was attrition and destruction not in the battle field but by damage and scars on the surface of the plates.

This can be seen around the edges extending into the pictures to obliterate parts of bodies and faces. The uncertainty and indiscriminate bad luck of a swath of black destroying part of a figure or a head seems as unfortunate as a stray bullet veering into a solider on the battlefield.

But most of the tintypes included here feel embattled, with distressed areas, smudges, blemishes and imperfections. These are not healthy pictures. They are compromised, as imperfect and unpredictable as the actual battles at Gettysburg. The pictures seem worn but the men pictured do not seem weary. In addition, my fingerprints are imprinted on the plates like clumsy signatures.

The wet plate process was consistent with its time, both culturally and temporally. Tintypes made in the field, like muskets needed to be loaded and shot one at a time; they required duration so much different than the instantaneous experience of time in the 21st century. The length of the exposures were significant because sitters had to compose themselves for the camera and ultimately for the future. Though some soldiers were positioned by Mathea the final act of composing was made by holding a posture and staring into the lens for 3 – 5 seconds. The act of holding still means to fashion a pose and expression and freezing it for the length of the exposure.

Unlike snapshots, moments from the flux of life, these are manufactured moments like a still life arrangement. It is a restrained experience and explains why so few historical pictures of people smiling exist because it feels so unnatural to" hold a smile". The several seconds to be still suspends time. There is no breathing in photographs. To be motionless is one way in nature to be invisible, but in these photographs it is to prepare for fixing oneself permanently on the plate, it is also a kind of practicing for death. Perhaps more here than any other time for the re-enactors because even falling on the battlefield, there is the head turning and watching until the skirmish or battle is over, and eventually getting up and walking back to camp.

Historically, pictures of soldiers during the civil war were made in encampments but also in temporary studios, this allowed for a standardization of backgrounds, props and lighting. The studio abolished all the vestiges of camp life and placed a premium on the props and staging. Photographs made in the camps show the fabric of life surrounding the soldiers: fields, forests, canvas tents, muskets, wool etc.; and the gestures, the space between soldiers, and the eyes.

In these photographs there is a shimmering between contemporary and historical. Muskets, canteens, tarps, glasses, shoes - the clothing and accessories of authentic period pieces. But the clothes seem fresh, unsoiled. And even in the heat and humidity the perspiration does not seem to have been soaking into the clothing for weeks. The bodies that fill up the wool trousers and shirts are contemporary. Men who are fed well on a sustained march though in the 21st century trying to make livings in the contemporary age, not a group of men bound to each other through the collective task of war. There are no eye sockets extruding, no wounds or signs of disease or distress. Instead we see bodies on average 53 pounds heavier than their counterparts 150 years ago. Though these pictures are simulated they are authentic, and honest. They acknowledge the original men of the 22nd North Carolina regiment. As mimicry is a form of flattery so re-enacting is a form of admiration, veneration and respect.

The value of a photograph changes when it is taken in the shadow of carnage and death. One has to assume that the tintype photograph, so new in the 1860s held a kind of magic that would preserve the solider and transcend its materials and token size. Photography was 24 years old in 1863. The ability to register the exact likeness of someone was astonishing. For soldiers photographed at the edges of battle the pictures must have been reassuring in their physical presence and permanence. 150 years later the photographs of the re-enactors function in a similar way, stand-ins from 6 generations later. The pictures show an impulse to stand in solidarity and unite on the surfaces of the pictures accommodating two times at once in the descriptions of the soldiers, the camps, and the light.

Keith Millman

PLATES

Colonel William Lee Joshua Lowrance

Colonel William Lee Joshua Lowrance was born on July 26, 1836 in Mooresville, North Carolina, the son of John Nichols Lowrance and Jane Kilpatrick. He attended Davidson College. Lowrance became a lieutenant in D company of the 34th North Carolina Regiment in September 1861, eventually rising to colonel by December 1862. He led the regiment in the brigade of Brigadier General William Dorsey Pender, part of MG A. P. Hill's Light Division at the Battle of Fredericksburg and possibly at the Battle of Chancellorsville. After Chancellorsville, Pender became division commander, and Brigadier General Alfred M. Scales took command of the brigade. At Gettysburg, Lowrance was wounded on the first day of fighting, but he later took command of the brigade in place of Scales, who had been severely wounded. Lowrance found the brigade sadly depleted, but he led it in Pickett's Charge on July 3, 1863. According to his report, the brigade and that of Brigadier General James H. Lane numbered no more than 800 troops. They advanced following the division led by Brigadier General J. Johnston Pettigrew, but they retreated upon finding themselves nearly alone in front of the federal line on Cemetery Ridge.

Colonel Lowrance returned to his regiment when General Scales rejoined the Army of Northern Virginia . Lowrance led the regiment in the Bristoe Campaign and the Mine Run Campaign. He fought in the Battle of the Wilderness and subsequent actions, including the earlier stages of the Siege of Petersburg. Colonel Lowrance led the brigade briefly when Scales was ill in late May 1864, including action at the Battle of North Anna. He led the brigade again when Scales was absent ill in November 1864. Lowrance went on sick leave on February 2, 1865 and did not return to the Army.

After the War, Lowrance was a merchant in Oxford, Mississippi and served in that state's legislature. In 1880, he moved to Texas and became a minister. He was the pastor of Oak Cliff Presbyterian Church in Dallas, Texas. Lowrance died in Forestville, Texas on March 24, 1916. He married Sarah C. Stewart in Atlanta, Georgia. They had four sons and two daughters.

Ken Snyder, age 66, is the Colonel of the 22nd North Carolina Regiment. He is a retired police officer from Baltimore, Maryland. Colonel Snyder knows the history of the Nineteenth Century regiment quite well.

"I was brought into re-enacting as a hobby by a forty-year friend of mine, Wayne Kellum. He was the original colonel. In 2005, he had a hip replacement and he got a blood clot. It took him. We formed the 22nd in honor of his ancestors. Before he passed, he left word that I should take command. I take that very seriously and we continue on in memory of his family members and in memory of him, and as long as I'm able to take the field I'll be here.

To me, the most important thing about re-enacting is the history and the camaraderie with my fellow partners. Equally as important is the passing on of the history to the younger generations. It is not taught in schools any longer. It's ancient history to them and it's left to us to do. I thoroughly enjoy having the children in camp and instructing children every opportunity I get.

It's a wonderful hobby. We welcome all comers. We'd love to have anybody who'd like to join the 22nd. We're a family group."

Sergeant John T. Reid

John T. Reid had previously served as Sergeant of this regiment before being promoted to Hospital Steward on October 9, 1861, and transferred to the Field and Staff. Present or accounted for until paroled at Appomattox Court House, Virginia, April 9, 1865.

John DeNoma, age 54, is the Major Surgeon of the 22nd North Carolina Regiment. Born in Pittsburg, Pennsylvania, he is an agronomist and currently lives in Orrtanda, Pennsylvania.

"I think re-enacting is important for several reasons. One is camaraderie. The second is to help keep history alive and hopefully spark the history bug with the youth today. Also, I provide modern medical support to the guys on the field. I'm a Pennsylvania emergency technician. I carry a trauma bag with me. Re-enactments serve a purpose in that we know people learn in different ways. Some people learn by reading, some people by experiencing hands on, and I think a major contribution of re-enacting is it's almost "immersion learning." And how better to remember and experience an issue than to do it yourself and have you better relate with the people that recorded their experiences in books. Now when I read anything on the Civil War, I have a whole new appreciation of being in battle, being in camp, the monotony, the adrenaline rushes, and the camaraderie.

When I joined the company I had just been in a horrible car accident and spent a year and a half in a body brace. I was wearing the brace when I met the "group" in front of the wax museum in Gettysburg. Ken Snyder stepped out of his comfort zone and said to me "Hey what happened? You seem interested. When you get all that crap off, why don't you come see us and we can make room for you?" Wayne Kellum was the same; he was open to all types, all people, kinda' bring you in. He had the ability to make it so you could all work together. It was one of his talents…. This is like being a grown up Boy Scout. I think I'm just a grown up kid. I take responsibility for my family and my job, but still we all have that pioneer in our heart, that trail blazer, in some way.

Re-enacting binds us because we are an eclectic group; I mean we all don't come from one walk of life. We all don't do the same thing. It's crazy what we do, from airplane mechanics to farmers to retired police officers, and I don't even know what some of our members do. It doesn't matter. It can bind the North to the South. Because I'm in the field of agriculture and I believe agriculture and culture in the south were combined. It was a way of life and I understand the long hours of hard work and the life style. Really, farming is a life style more than anything else because you change your way of living to accommodate your labors. In the south there wasn't industry; it wasn't all CEOs of companies. It was people who had to work and fight for everything they had. And they had to fight nature, which is sometimes the toughest."

Captain Gaston V. Lamb

Captain Gaston V. Lamb resided in Randolph County, where he enlisted at age 24, June 5, 1861. Mustered in as Sergeant and was elected 2nd Lieutenant on May 1, 1862. Wounded in the leg at Mechanicsville, Virginia, June 26, 1862. Promoted to Captain on July 18, 1862. Wounded in both thighs at Chancellorsville, Virginia, May 1-4, 1863. Wounded at Gettysburg, Pennsylvania, July 1-3, 1863. Wounded in the left leg at or near Jericho Mills, Virginia, on or about May 23, 1864. Returned to duty in September-October, 1864. Paroled at Appomattox Court House, Virginia, April 9, 1865.

Henry Rathbone, age 49, is a Captain of the 22nd North Carolina Regiment. Born and raised in Canton, North Carolina; his family has lived there since 1790. He is an assistant manager at Car Quest Auto Parts.

"I've been a re-enactor for twenty-five years. Just plain out, it's fun. There's nothing else like it. The main reason I re-enact is for my ancestors. Ever since I was a kid I've loved history. Haywood County is up in the mountains of North Carolina and I'm related to a big chunk of the population there. Everybody you know. I mean you just walk across the ridge and marry somebody. I couldn't even tell you right now the number of people that I'm related to, and many that served this country. There's 39 of them in Haywood County. At Gettysburg, the 22nd North Carolina was part of Scales' brigade. It had never been stopped in an attack before and there were many engagements before Gettysburg. They went into that battle on the first day some 1,400 men strong, and only about 500 of them answered present for duty when it was over. Every field officer save one was down. They still went in on the third day and crossed the wall, what was left of them. Those men were… I just can't, there is too much. We want people to see that these men believed in why they were there. The huge overbearing federal government we've got today sticking its finger in every little section of our lives is the true legacy of that war. My ancestors lived up in the mountains on little subsistence farms. After the war they lived as sharecroppers; most of them didn't have anything left.

They weren't out there risking life and limb in performing feats like that so some rich fellow down in flat country could keep his slaves. Yes, it was an issue, but that wasn't why they were there. They were there for the right to self-determination. They believed that they had a right to a government that established justice; like for those things that they should decide whether or not they could cut down a tree in the back yard, or whether or not, you know what I'm saying? I've always believed that those men were there to protect their homes, their families, and their freedoms. You can imagine, most of them probably sat on grandpa's knee and listened to him tell how they fought the British to get that freedom and now somebody up North wanted to take some of that away and they weren't about to give that up, especially not when they decide to invade 'em. Taxation without representation was the big thing back in the Revolution, and by the time we came up to this stage there were more Northern people in Congress than there were Southern people, and it was starting to change. Most of the money the government took in was from the tariffs, and port taxes and stuff. That went to Washington where Congress decided where to spend it. Most of the money coming out of southern pockets was spent somewhere else. And that was an issue. In 1857 in the Senate, Abraham Lincoln said that if the government did not suit a man, he should rise and shake it off and form a new one that suited him better. You can look that up. Soon, as he became president he was determined to control all states' power. Lincoln said I need some 75,000 men to stop this insurrection…. One way or the other, I think those issues are unresolved to this day."

Captain William B. Gooding

Captain William B. Gooding resided in McDowell County where he enlisted at age 23, June 5, 1861. Mustered in as 1st Sergeant and was elected 2nd Lieutenant on May, 1862. Promoted to 1st Lieutenant on September 6, 1862, and was promoted to Captain on December 1, 1862. Wounded in the left arm at Gettysburg, Pennsylvania, July 1, 1863. Left arm amputated. Resigned on December 12, 1863, by reason of disability. Later served as Commandant of the 10th Congressional District of North Carolina.

Tony Miller, age 52, is a Captain of the 22nd North Carolina Regiment. Born and raised in Ohio he and his family currently reside in Bowling Green, Ohio. He is a customer service representative.

"I've been a re-enactor for twelve years. I am often asked why a man born and raised in Ohio joined a Confederate infantry re-enactor's regiment? The reason is I had ancestors on both sides. I first got interested when I was nine years old. My mom and grandmother took me to see "Gone with the Wind" in the theater and I was hooked. We had sympathy for the South because my maternal grandmother was from Georgia. My paternal side came from Tennessee. She always filled me with Confederate stories about Robert E Lee and our ancestors. They didn't have any losses from the war; they all came back. I also had ancestors in the 52nd Ohio and I know they all came back.

I think re-enactments serve a purpose because the history that is taught in schools today is not complete. There is no in-depth analysis of history. It's basically glossed over and it's revisionist always. The phrase that the victor always writes the history is true and the more you study history the more you find out that is true. I'm sure the US has done that with the war with Germany, and the war with Japan. (Real analysis requires the German and Japanese viewpoints.) So what we do here in encampments reminds the general public of that (mid nineteenth-century) time period and the issues that are still active today: state's rights, racism, self-government. These are still topics in the news today. What we do is try to portray as accurately as possible, not just the military life, but the camp life itself. People might read that in books or see it on TV, but they don't see guys cleaning their muskets, or them cooking over a fire. They don't see us in the "down time" telling jokes, playing cards, or whatever we're doing. They don't see that. All they see is the action and the battle. And re-enacting is personally fulfilling. You have to have a passion, and I think everyone here loves what they are doing. You get to turn off the phone. You don't have to listen to the crap on TV. You don't have to hear whatever kind of music you don't like. A lot of people don't like what you hear in the background, the fife and drum, but it's a nice change. No, I wouldn't want to listen to it every day, all day long. You can forget about the stress and the hurry up of the modern world. You know, gotta' be here now, gotta' go, gotta' be on time."

Lieutenant Joseph B. Clark

Lieutenant Joseph B. Clark resided in Caldwell County where he enlisted at age 24. Elected 2nd Lieutenant on April 30, 1861, and was elected 1st Lieutenant on August 8, 1861. Defeated for reelection on May 10, 1862; however, he was appointed 2nd Lieutenant on May 30, 1862. Appointed 1st Lieutenant on October 28, 1862. Wounded in the right arm at Gettysburg, Pennsylvania, July 1- 3, 1863. Returned to duty on or about July 31, 1863 and was present or accounted for through October 1864.

Gary Story, age 44, is a Lieutenant in the 22nd North Carolina regiment. He was born and raised in North Carolina, and is a textile worker.

"I have been a re-enactor for several years, and I re-enact mostly to preserve the history and remember my relatives. I had several ancestors who fought in the war. They gave up so much. I am familiar with the history of the regiment in the Battle of Gettysburg, but they were in different units. Specifically at this battle I lost a lot of relatives. A lot were wounded and captured so when you come to a big event like this (the 150th anniversary of the Battle of Gettysburg, with nearly 10,000 re-enactors,) it's kind of personal. I do think that re-enacting serves a purpose. It preserves the history. It preserves the sacrifices these men went through. They had a belief and they weren't willing to back down. I re-enact, personally, for another reason. It's the brotherhood. We're all, we're like family. Ya' know, sometimes we share each other's hard times. Just to have somebody to talk to. We share food, stories. It's just like being with a family, you know? It's hard to explain other than it's like family."

Sergeant Pickens Barlow

Sergeant Pickens Barlow was born in Caldwell County where he resided as a farmer prior to enlisting in Caldwell County at age 23, April 30, 1861. Mustered in as a private. Wounded at Seven Pines, Virginia, May 31, 1862. Promoted to Sergeant on June 10, 1862. Wounded in the neck at Fredericksburg, Virginia, December 13, 1862. Wounded and captured at Gettysburg, Pennsylvania, July 1-4, 1863. Hospitalized at David's Island, New York Harbor, until paroled and transferred to City Point, Virginia where he was received September 16, 1863 for exchange. Returned to duty prior to September 1, 1864 and was present or accounted for until paroled at Appomattox court House, Virginia, April 9, 1865.

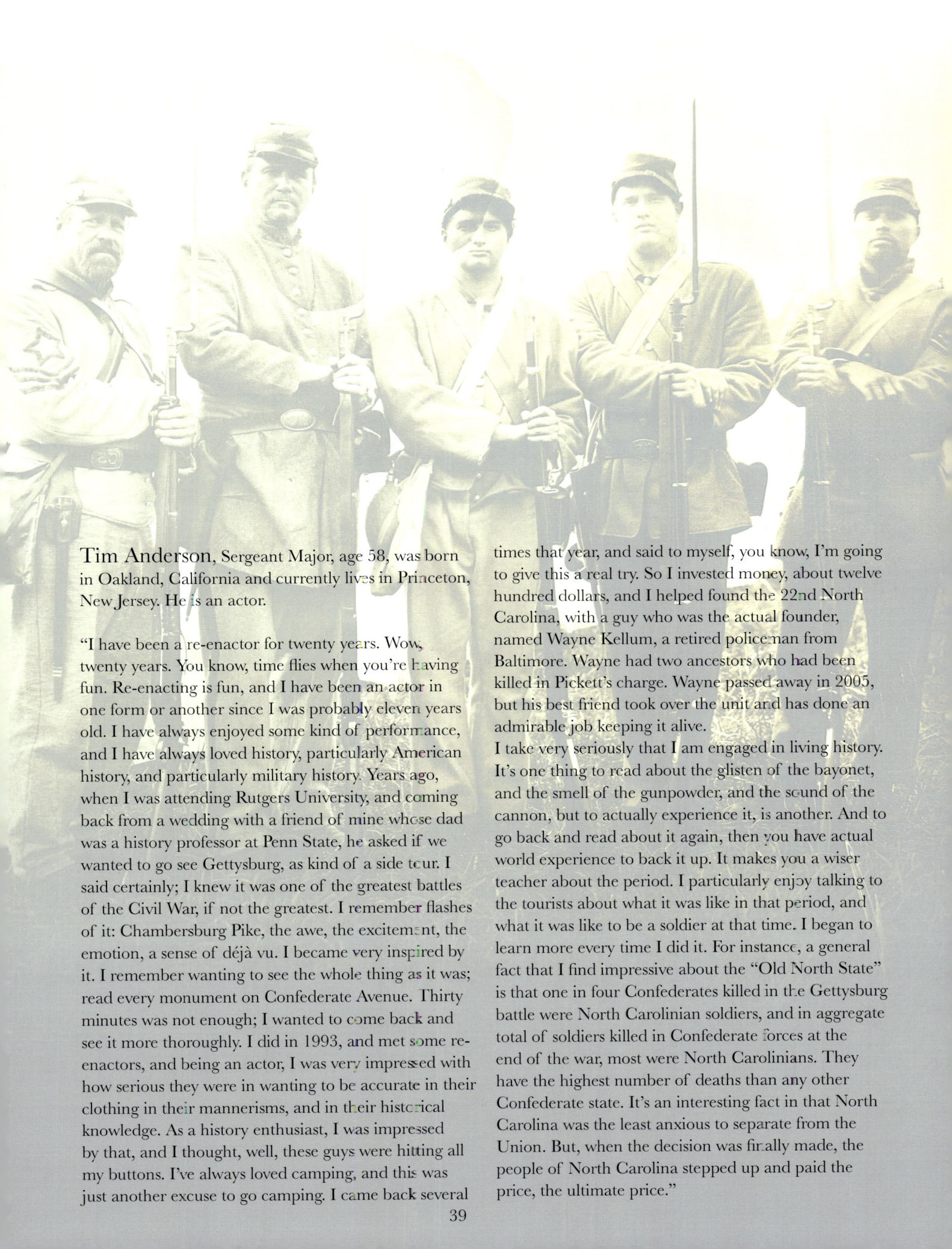

Tim Anderson, Sergeant Major, age 58, was born in Oakland, California and currently lives in Princeton, New Jersey. He is an actor.

"I have been a re-enactor for twenty years. Wow, twenty years. You know, time flies when you're having fun. Re-enacting is fun, and I have been an actor in one form or another since I was probably eleven years old. I have always enjoyed some kind of performance, and I have always loved history, particularly American history, and particularly military history. Years ago, when I was attending Rutgers University, and coming back from a wedding with a friend of mine whose dad was a history professor at Penn State, he asked if we wanted to go see Gettysburg, as kind of a side tour. I said certainly; I knew it was one of the greatest battles of the Civil War, if not the greatest. I remember flashes of it: Chambersburg Pike, the awe, the excitement, the emotion, a sense of déjà vu. I became very inspired by it. I remember wanting to see the whole thing as it was; read every monument on Confederate Avenue. Thirty minutes was not enough; I wanted to come back and see it more thoroughly. I did in 1993, and met some re-enactors, and being an actor, I was very impressed with how serious they were in wanting to be accurate in their clothing in their mannerisms, and in their historical knowledge. As a history enthusiast, I was impressed by that, and I thought, well, these guys were hitting all my buttons. I've always loved camping, and this was just another excuse to go camping. I came back several

times that year, and said to myself, you know, I'm going to give this a real try. So I invested money, about twelve hundred dollars, and I helped found the 22nd North Carolina, with a guy who was the actual founder, named Wayne Kellum, a retired policeman from Baltimore. Wayne had two ancestors who had been killed in Pickett's charge. Wayne passed away in 2005, but his best friend took over the unit and has done an admirable job keeping it alive.

I take very seriously that I am engaged in living history. It's one thing to read about the glisten of the bayonet, and the smell of the gunpowder, and the sound of the cannon, but to actually experience it, is another. And to go back and read about it again, then you have actual world experience to back it up. It makes you a wiser teacher about the period. I particularly enjoy talking to the tourists about what it was like in that period, and what it was like to be a soldier at that time. I began to learn more every time I did it. For instance, a general fact that I find impressive about the "Old North State" is that one in four Confederates killed in the Gettysburg battle were North Carolinian soldiers, and in aggregate total of soldiers killed in Confederate forces at the end of the war, most were North Carolinians. They have the highest number of deaths than any other Confederate state. It's an interesting fact in that North Carolina was the least anxious to separate from the Union. But, when the decision was finally made, the people of North Carolina stepped up and paid the price, the ultimate price."

Sergeant James E. Campbell

Sergeant James E. Campbell was born in Randolph County where he resided as a blacksmith prior to enlisting in Randolph County at age 22, March 6, 1862. Mustered in as a Private and was promoted to Corporal prior to May 28, 1862. Wounded and captured at Gettysburg, Pennsylvania, July 1-3, 1863. Hospitalized at Chester, Pennsylvania, until transferred to Point Lookout, Maryland, where he arrived October 4, 1863. Paroled at Point Lookout and transferred to City Point, Virginia, where he was received March 6, 12864, for exchange. Returned to duty on an unspecified date and was promoted to Sergeant prior to September 1, 1864. Retired to Invalid Corps on November 17, 1864, by reason of disability. Paroled at Greensboro on May 17, 1865.

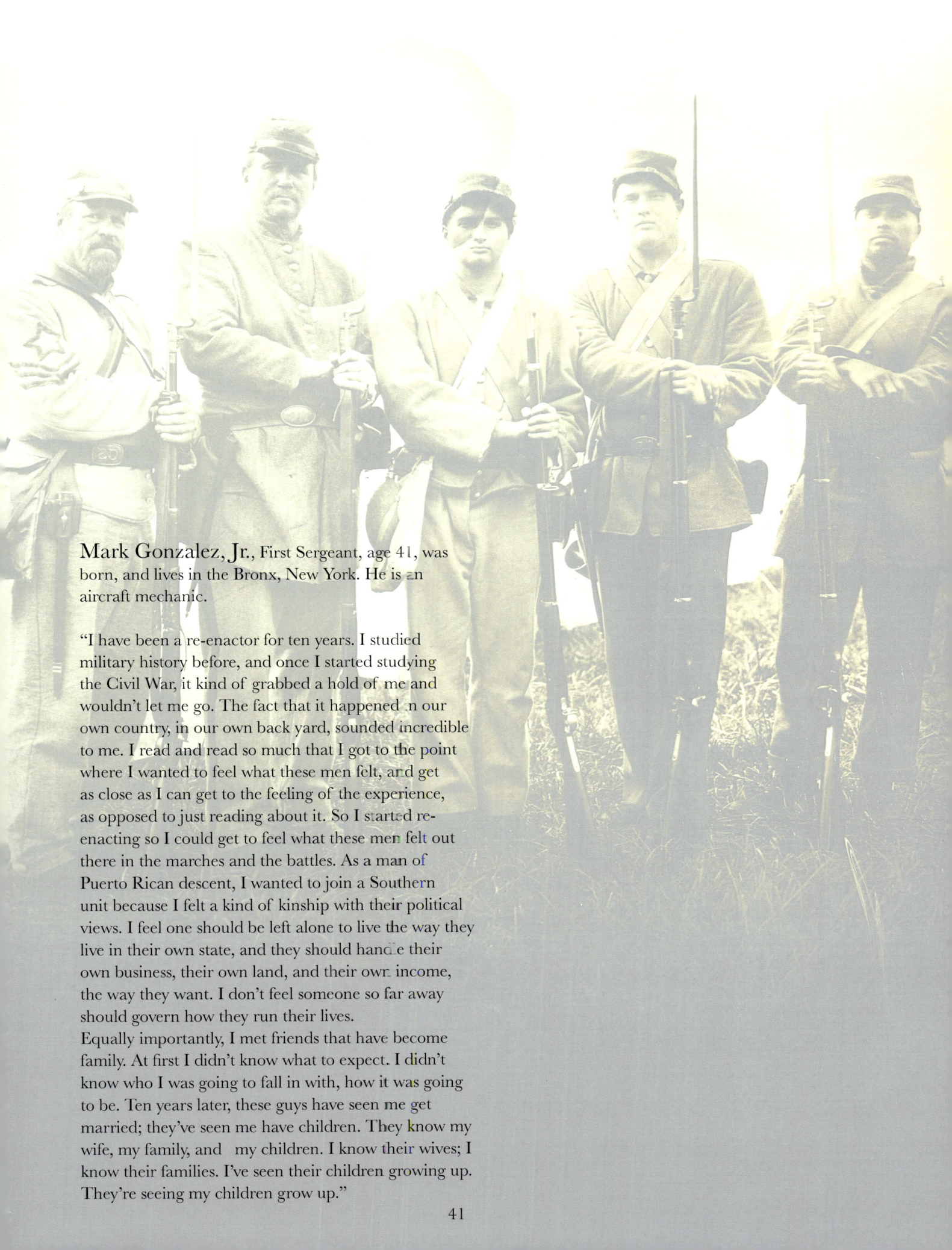

Mark Gonzalez, Jr., First Sergeant, age 41, was born, and lives in the Bronx, New York. He is an aircraft mechanic.

"I have been a re-enactor for ten years. I studied military history before, and once I started studying the Civil War, it kind of grabbed a hold of me and wouldn't let me go. The fact that it happened in our own country, in our own back yard, sounded incredible to me. I read and read so much that I got to the point where I wanted to feel what these men felt, and get as close as I can get to the feeling of the experience, as opposed to just reading about it. So I started re-enacting so I could get to feel what these men felt out there in the marches and the battles. As a man of Puerto Rican descent, I wanted to join a Southern unit because I felt a kind of kinship with their political views. I feel one should be left alone to live the way they live in their own state, and they should handle their own business, their own land, and their own income, the way they want. I don't feel someone so far away should govern how they run their lives.
Equally importantly, I met friends that have become family. At first I didn't know what to expect. I didn't know who I was going to fall in with, how it was going to be. Ten years later, these guys have seen me get married; they've seen me have children. They know my wife, my family, and my children. I know their wives; I know their families. I've seen their children growing up. They're seeing my children grow up."

41

Sergeant Stephen Trogdon

Sergeant Stephen Trogdon resided in Randolph County where he enlisted at age 24, June 10 1861. Mustered in as Private and was promoted to Corporal on December 13, 1862. Captured at Fredericksburg, Virginia, December 13, 1862. Exchanged on December 17, 1862. Promoted to Sergeant prior to July 1, 1863. Wounded in the right thigh and captured at Gettysburg, Pennsylvania, July 1-3, 1863. Right leg amputated. Hospitalized at David's Island, New York Harbor, until paroled and transferred to City Point, Virginia, where he was received October 28, 1863, for exchange. Retired to the Invalid Corps on August 13, 1864.

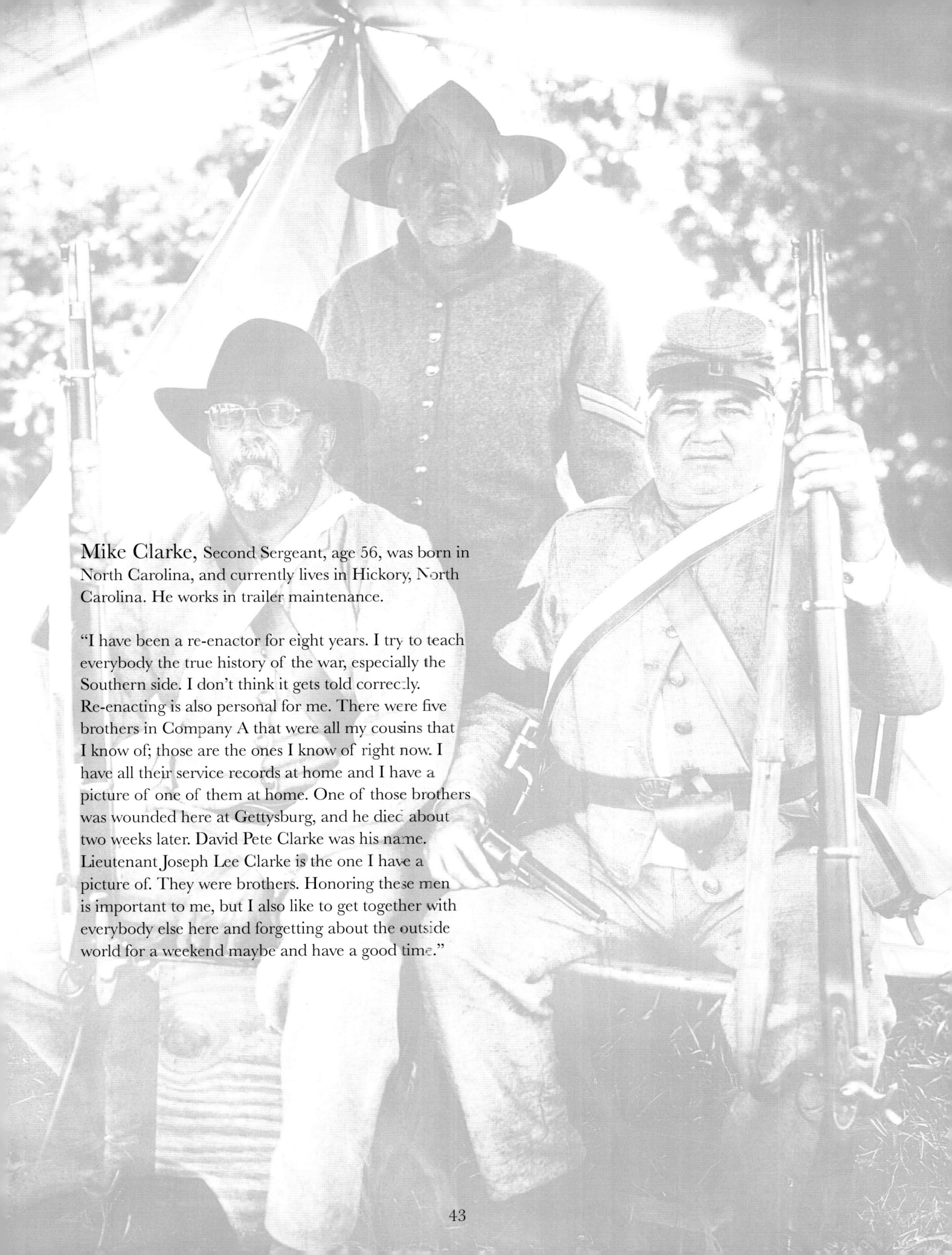

Mike Clarke, Second Sergeant, age 56, was born in North Carolina, and currently lives in Hickory, North Carolina. He works in trailer maintenance.

"I have been a re-enactor for eight years. I try to teach everybody the true history of the war, especially the Southern side. I don't think it gets told correctly. Re-enacting is also personal for me. There were five brothers in Company A that were all my cousins that I know of; those are the ones I know of right now. I have all their service records at home and I have a picture of one of them at home. One of those brothers was wounded here at Gettysburg, and he died about two weeks later. David Pete Clarke was his name. Lieutenant Joseph Lee Clarke is the one I have a picture of. They were brothers. Honoring these men is important to me, but I also like to get together with everybody else here and forgetting about the outside world for a weekend maybe and have a good time."

Sergeant William Garvin

Sergeant William Garvin resided in McDowell County where he enlisted at age 20, May 8, 1861. Mustered as Private and was promoted to Sergeant in February, 1863. Wounded and captured at Gettysburg, Pennsylvania, July 1-3, 1863. Hospitalized at David's Island, New York Harbor, until paroled and transferred to City Point, Virginia, where he was received September 16, 1864, for exchange. Company records do not indicate whether he returned to duty; however, he was paroled at Greensboro on May 20, 1865.

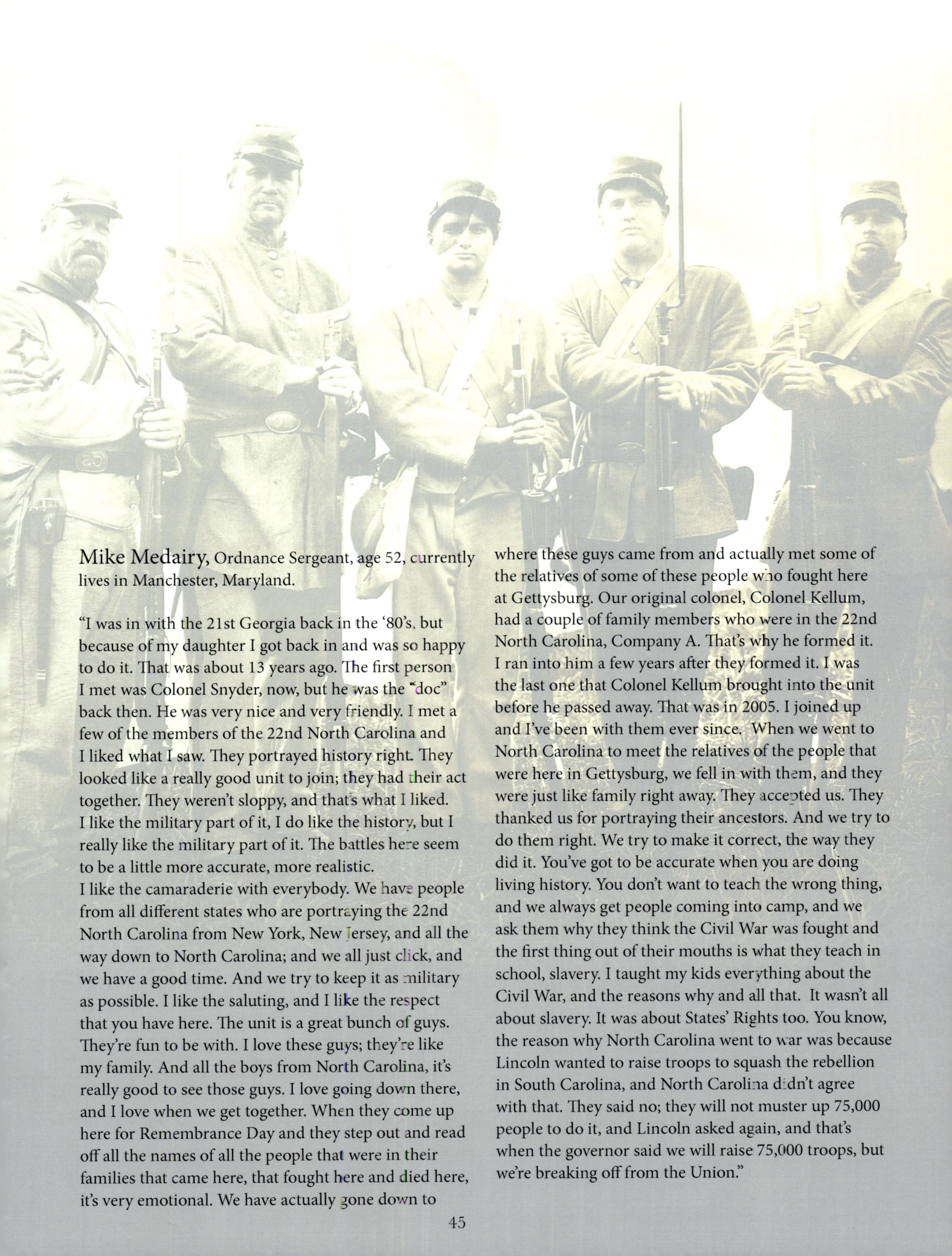

Mike Medairy, Ordnance Sergeant, age 52, currently lives in Manchester, Maryland.

"I was in with the 21st Georgia back in the '80's, but because of my daughter I got back in and was so happy to do it. That was about 13 years ago. The first person I met was Colonel Snyder, now, but he was the "doc" back then. He was very nice and very friendly. I met a few of the members of the 22nd North Carolina and I liked what I saw. They portrayed history right. They looked like a really good unit to join; they had their act together. They weren't sloppy, and that's what I liked. I like the military part of it, I do like the history, but I really like the military part of it. The battles here seem to be a little more accurate, more realistic.

I like the camaraderie with everybody. We have people from all different states who are portraying the 22nd North Carolina from New York, New Jersey, and all the way down to North Carolina; and we all just click, and we have a good time. And we try to keep it as military as possible. I like the saluting, and I like the respect that you have here. The unit is a great bunch of guys. They're fun to be with. I love these guys; they're like my family. And all the boys from North Carolina, it's really good to see those guys. I love going down there, and I love when we get together. When they come up here for Remembrance Day and they step out and read off all the names of all the people that were in their families that came here, that fought here and died here, it's very emotional. We have actually gone down to where these guys came from and actually met some of the relatives of some of these people who fought here at Gettysburg. Our original colonel, Colonel Kellum, had a couple of family members who were in the 22nd North Carolina, Company A. That's why he formed it. I ran into him a few years after they formed it. I was the last one that Colonel Kellum brought into the unit before he passed away. That was in 2005. I joined up and I've been with them ever since. When we went to North Carolina to meet the relatives of the people that were here in Gettysburg, we fell in with them, and they were just like family right away. They accepted us. They thanked us for portraying their ancestors. And we try to do them right. We try to make it correct, the way they did it. You've got to be accurate when you are doing living history. You don't want to teach the wrong thing, and we always get people coming into camp, and we ask them why they think the Civil War was fought and the first thing out of their mouths is what they teach in school, slavery. I taught my kids everything about the Civil War, and the reasons why and all that. It wasn't all about slavery. It was about States' Rights too. You know, the reason why North Carolina went to war was because Lincoln wanted to raise troops to squash the rebellion in South Carolina, and North Carolina didn't agree with that. They said no; they will not muster up 75,000 people to do it, and Lincoln asked again, and that's when the governor said we will raise 75,000 troops, but we're breaking off from the Union."

First Sergeant Marcus Deal

First Sergeant Marcus Deal resided in Caldwell County where he enlisted at age 23, April 30, 1861. Mustered in as private. Transferred to Company M of this regiment on an unspecified date subsequent to August 31, 1861. Transferred back to this company in July 1862, while absent wounded. Reported absent wounded through October 1862. Promoted to Corporal in November.

Tony Panou, Sergeant, age 49, was born in Charlotte, North Carolina, and currently lives in Marion, North Carolina. He is both a short order cook and a restaurant operator.

"I've been a re-enactor for seven years in the 22nd North Carolina regiment. It's very important. A lot of people, especially down in the South, still live the Civil War. They feel betrayed and that's the memory that, even though it's bitter, they don't let it go. They are proud of their men who served in the Civil War, and the women. It's important for us to be able say we represent a certain group of people that today we're connected to, because geographically they are our ancestral blood lines. A lot of the families had their men go off to war, so what was left was women and children to fend for the farms, the animals, and the children, and the Federals would come through here, not necessarily Yankees. Some were North Carolinians that turned blue coat and were sent right back into western North Carolina to pillage and steal anything they needed without any questions being asked. I know a lot about the 22nd North Carolina regiment. A lot of these people who made it back have living descendants who are proud to mention their names and talk about their adventures during the Civil War. A lot of them didn't make it to the end. They were furloughed, were sent home early because they were sick or too old. They had families to take care of, farms to take care of, and animals. Some actually left the war, just disappeared, because they wanted to go back home because there were Federals around our area and a lot of them just left their regiment and went back home to protect their property, their, crops, and land, their livelihood and their families.

Representing these men as re-enactors, we're looked at as maybe, to some degree, as living historians. Because I run a business and work a lot with the public, everybody that eats at my place knows I'm a re-enactor and they admire that. The war wasn't a good time for anybody. The results were not favorable in the end for both parties. But, there is a great sense of pride in the re-enactors and what they do. A lot of them have ancestors that were in a place like this. It's a great feeling I feel proud to be able to represent a small group of ethnic ancestors that I would call Greek that served with the Confederacy. There were about fifty. Even today in McDowell County, and in other counties, we still remember these people with graveyard dedications, and other remembrances."

47

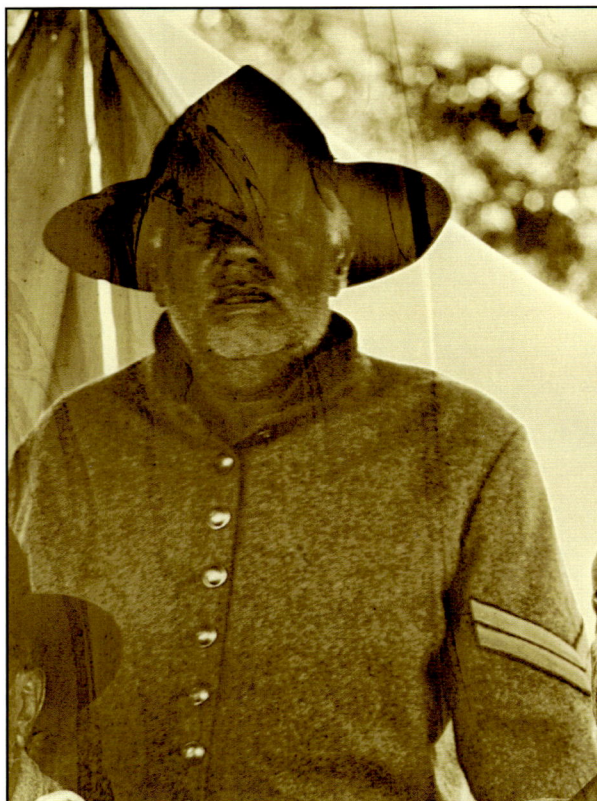

Corporal Lewis M. Dinkins

Corporal Lewis M. Dinkins was born in Caldwell County where he resided as a carpenter prior to enlisting in Caldwell County at age 23, April 30, 1861. Mustered in as a Corporal. Wounded in an unspecified battle in September 1862. Captured at Gettysburg, Pennsylvania, July 1-3, 1863. Confined at Fort Delaware, Delaware, until transferred to Point Lookout, Maryland, October 15, 1863. Released at Point Lookout on February 10, 1864, after taking the Oath of Allegiance and joining the U.S. Army. Assigned to Company G, 1st Regiment U.S. Volunteer Infantry.

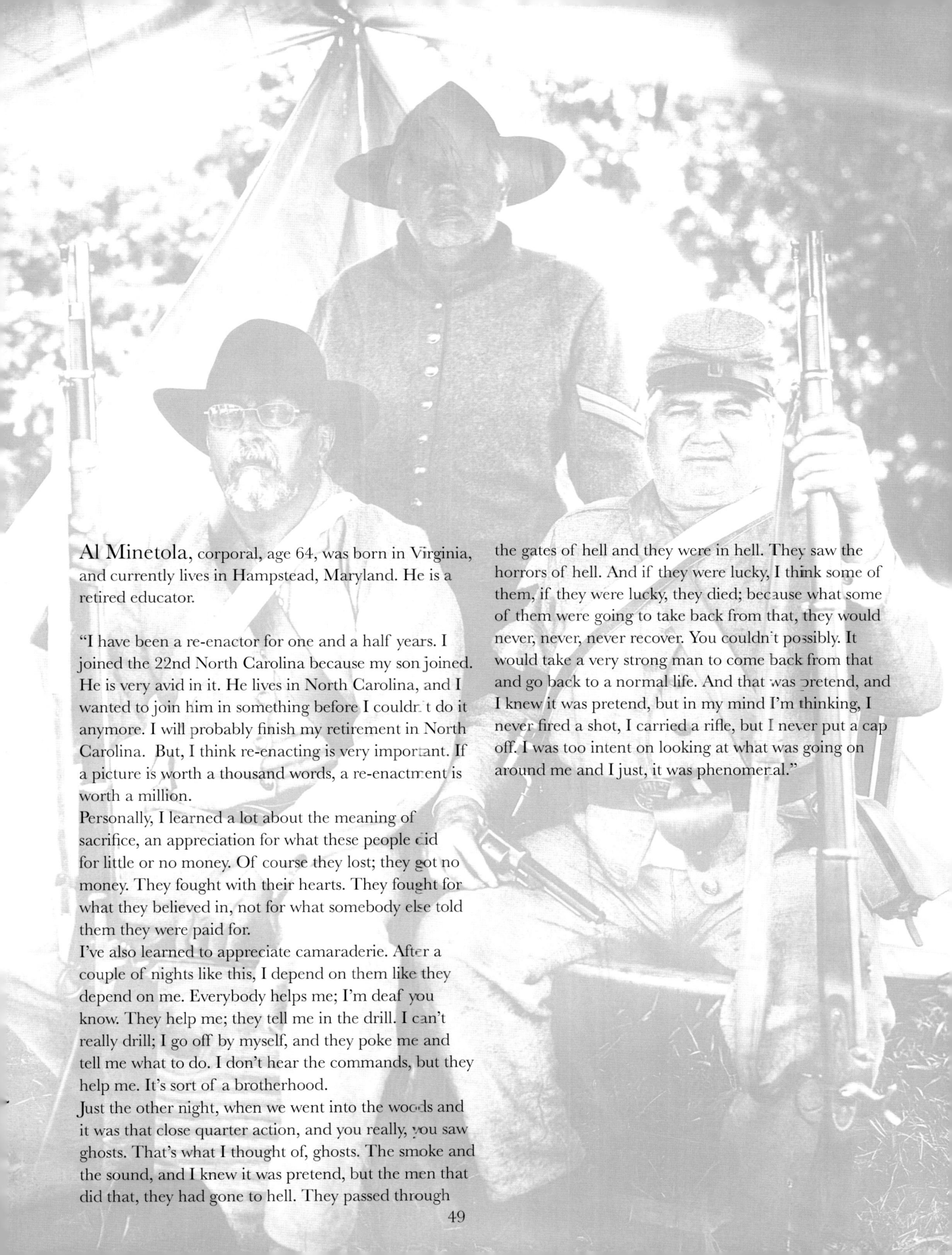

Al Minetola, corporal, age 64, was born in Virginia, and currently lives in Hampstead, Maryland. He is a retired educator.

"I have been a re-enactor for one and a half years. I joined the 22nd North Carolina because my son joined. He is very avid in it. He lives in North Carolina, and I wanted to join him in something before I couldn't do it anymore. I will probably finish my retirement in North Carolina. But, I think re-enacting is very important. If a picture is worth a thousand words, a re-enactment is worth a million.

Personally, I learned a lot about the meaning of sacrifice, an appreciation for what these people did for little or no money. Of course they lost; they got no money. They fought with their hearts. They fought for what they believed in, not for what somebody else told them they were paid for.

I've also learned to appreciate camaraderie. After a couple of nights like this, I depend on them like they depend on me. Everybody helps me; I'm deaf you know. They help me; they tell me in the drill. I can't really drill; I go off by myself, and they poke me and tell me what to do. I don't hear the commands, but they help me. It's sort of a brotherhood.

Just the other night, when we went into the woods and it was that close quarter action, and you really, you saw ghosts. That's what I thought of, ghosts. The smoke and the sound, and I knew it was pretend, but the men that did that, they had gone to hell. They passed through the gates of hell and they were in hell. They saw the horrors of hell. And if they were lucky, I think some of them, if they were lucky, they died; because what some of them were going to take back from that, they would never, never, never recover. You couldn't possibly. It would take a very strong man to come back from that and go back to a normal life. And that was pretend, and I knew it was pretend, but in my mind I'm thinking, I never fired a shot, I carried a rifle, but I never put a cap off. I was too intent on looking at what was going on around me and I just, it was phenomenal."

49

Corporal Pleasant B. Hennis

Corporal Pleasant B. Hennis resided in Stokes County where he enlisted at age 20, June 1, 1861. Mustered in as Private. Transferred to Company F of this regiment in September 1861-May, 1862. Transferred back to this company on July 1, 1862. Transferred back to this company on July 1, 1862. Wounded in both knees at the Second Battle of Manassas, Virginia, August 29-30, 2862. Reported absent wounded through October 1862. Company records do not indicate whether he returned to duty; however he was hospitalized at Danville, Virginia, June 26, 1863 with a gunshot wound. Place and date wounded not reported. Returned to duty on July 1, 1863, and was promoted to Corporal in July 1863-June 1864. Reported absent wounded on June 20, 1864. Place and date wounded not reported. Returned to duty in September-October 1864. Present or accounted for through October 1864.

Eric Minetola, corporal, age 40, was born in Pennsylvania and currently lives in Morganton, North Carolina.

"I've been a re-enactor for twenty years. I do it because it's an important way to teach history. By studying history, and re-enacting it, I'm teaching like I'm in school. I enjoy learning history this way. I had a lot of teachers that were re-enactors. I think the hands-on learning way of teaching is the best. You can touch it. You can feel it. You can smell it. It's really good. Yes I think it gives realism. It's more than a book. You know we always joke about the sense of smell. It's the sound. I don't think you'd actually want to see the real thing, but this is as close as you can get. Who was it that said: "War is not the answer; young men shouldn't die?" I agree. I think that's a really good lesson that people need to take out of re-enacting. You need to learn to talk, and not fight. War is not the best answer to America's problems. You know, I was born and raised in Pennsylvania; graduated college in Pennsylvania, then moved to North Carolina right after I got married in 1998. Up until that point, I had re-enacted in two groups in Pennsylvania. When I moved south, I kinda' got out of it for a little while; but, I would take this stuff into school and work with the kids. I didn't really do a lot of this kind of stuff. Then I started my Master's classes and I needed something to get away from the stress of the classes and the stress of the classroom, so I started back up again.

I do not know of any members of my family that fought in the war. My mom's side of the family is Pennsylvania German. My dad's side of the family came from Italy in 1906. I don't have any real problems with re-enacting from the North or the South. Having learned as "Blue, "I prefer the "Blue," but it doesn't really bother me. Some people take it very seriously. I believe in learning both sides, presenting both sides, and teaching both sides. I do get teased for being a "Yankee," but in reality, I've made a lot of friends. I love the camaraderie with the other guys. It's great for relaxation and stress relief. It's also a vacation, sort of back in time. It gets you out."

Private John H. Dale, Jr

Private John H. Dale, Jr was born in McDowell County where he resided as a farmer prior to enlisting in McDowell County at age 23, March 16, 1862. Wounded in the left leg at Gettysburg, Pennsylvania, July 1, 1863. Left leg amputated on July 2, 1863. Captured at Gettysburg on July 5, 1863. Hospitalized at Chester, Pennsylvania, until paroled and transferred to City Point, Virginia, September 17, 1863, for exchange. Retired to the Invalid Corps on July 29, 1864.

Lance Carroll, private, age 56, was born in Bethesda, Maryland and currently lives in Springfield, Virginia. He is a businessman.

"I have been a re-enactor, on and off, for over forty years. I was a military brat that moved a lot, and I also served for twenty-six years. I went to college in North Carolina, and was stationed at Fort Bragg, North Carolina for ten years, so I've got fourteen years in North Carolina. That's why, as a re-enactor, the 22nd North Carolina was attractive to me.

I became a re-enactor because I have been a Civil War buff since I was knee high to a grasshopper, that is, since I was very young. I started collecting Civil War relics when I was ten to twelve years old. I used to mow yards to buy things like buckles and bullets. Back in those days you could still use metal detectors find stuff, so I did that. For the last thirty years, I also volunteer one day a week at the Arlington House at the Arlington National Cemetery, where Robert E Lee married into the house of Miss Mary Ann Custis.

Due to my military experience, I became a re-enactor also to experience what the men of the time experienced, and to help immortalize the soldiers who fought during the war. It is a way of keeping their memories alive. It's a venue for us that enjoy doing this, that we can do this. There's a little bit of sanity to it, so we can justify it to our wives, our loved ones and our kids as to why at forty, fifty, and sixty years old we are still out there running around in uniforms. It kind of supplements the stacks of books that are sitting on all the coffee tables in the house about the Civil War. Re-enacting allows me to teach. I enjoy sharing what I've learned, but it forces me to learn more. So it's an education process for me. Also, as I study the unit and as I study the dress of the time, I try to get into the mindset of the time, both from a personal, as well as a strategic perspective, of what was going on in our nation at that time and how to translate that to an individual soldier. But mostly, I re-enact to continue the legacy of the men who fought and enjoy the camaraderie of people with similar interests."

Private Aurelius James Dula

Private Aurelius James Dula resided in Caldwell County where he enlisted at age 18, April 30, 1861. Wounded in the arm at Gaines' Mills Virginia, June 27, 1862. Reported absent wounded through July 1862. Returned to duty on an unspecified date. Wounded in the right foot, right leg, and left arm at Gettysburg, Pennsylvania, July 1-3, 1863. Returned to duty on an unspecified date and was captured on the Jerusalem Plank Road, near Petersburg, Virginia, June 22, 1864. Confined at Point Lookout, Maryland, until paroled and transferred to Boulware's and Cox's Wharves, James River, Virginia, where he was received February 20-21, 1865, for exchange.

Craig Carroll, private, age 65, was born in North Carolina and currently lives in Ashland, Virginia. He has worked on historical films and TV programs, and is currently retired.

"I have been a re-enactor for forty years. I have represented every rank from colonel on down. Back in the 70's I commanded just about all the Confederate units back for about two years. Then I had a store, and so I just didn't have the time. I went back to private, but I got out for several years. Just needed to make a living. I think I got caught up in reading and researching these people and I think people like myself realized the sacrifices that made our great nation, so I wanted to learn more, and began re-enacting. In some way, we are all historians and are able to study just about all the regiments that participated in the war. They were aware they were making history and there is regimental history for almost every Union and Confederate unit, regiment, division, brigade, corp. This unit, the 22nd, was one of the few units that actually crossed the stone wall at Picket's Charge. They went the furthest and suffered horrendous casualties, and they lost their battle flag here. And to lose their flag was like losing the seal of their state or your community. They were very state oriented and the flag represented everything to these soldiers, both North and South.

Re-enacting is very important because it teaches American history. This is called living history. The battles are great. Nobody actually dies in them, but we portray that. It's more about giving the general public, the Neophytes as we call them, what it was all about. You can read the books and see the movies but to actually come and see one of these events and smell the campfires and the black powder smoke and see these people who come from all over the United States to honor our ancestors brings it all to life. For a lot of these guys, their ancestors were in those units. Our ancestor was a Union soldier in the 14th Michigan; he was not in the East. He fought out west at Shiloh and was cited for bravery at Chickamauga. He was a sergeant named Patrick Lee Carroll. I named my son after him, who is currently serving in Afghanistan. Actually what I think I get the most out of in re-enacting, is fellowship. Just coming out here again, after so many years; it's amazing to come back and see people my age. First thing you say is "my gosh, you've really aged." But, we have a good time and the fellowship and taking the time to talk to the younger generation. That is probably one of the most important things about re-enacting, to continue with it so it doesn't die off. Back in the early days, when I was commanding all the Confederates, we actually fought on the original battlefields. I was an historian for the Park Service for Fredericksburg. I'd allow them to come down to the parks and fight it out in the Wilderness and Chancellorsville Battlefields; of course you can't do that today. But things and time change all that."

Private Elisha A. Guyer

Private Elisha A. Guyer enlisted in Guilford County at age 19, February 22, 1862. Wounded at Gettysburg, Pennsylvania, July 1-3, 1863. Wounded at or near Spotsylvania Court House, Virginia, on or about May 20, 1864. Reported absent wounded until October 1, 1864, when he was reported absent without leave. Paroled at Greensboro on May 20, 1865.

Mark Ragan, private, age 56, was born in North Carolina and currently lives in Maryland. He is a researcher.

"I've re-enacted, on and off, from 1972 to the present. I now re-enact to recapture my youth. Really, I do it to honor my family. My grandmother on my father's side is all North Carolinian. So when I do the re-enactment stuff, I like the North Carolinian stuff anyway. My father's mother's side was actually in the 24th North Carolina. These guys are from a little further west in the state. I had a lot of relatives in the war actually; some captured, and some fought up until the end of the whole thing. My great-great-grandfather was killed in the war. So I have a soft spot for the North Carolinians. But, as re-enactors, we also go Yankee just because we have to be fair. Look, you gotta' bite the bullet occasionally and you gotta' put on that blue uniform. But, when you're playing a Yankee, everybody else looks just like you and you can't stand out. It's difficult, I mean, when you see a really, really authentic Union soldier, just like when you see a really, really authentic Confederate soldier. They do stand out,   but they are a lot rarer in the Union ranks because everybody pretty much has the same equipment. You're camping out and all this, and can't wear a feather in your hat playing a Yankee, but you can as a Confederate and that's the difference. You can have a little more personal flair in a Confederate uniform than a Union uniform because it's all GI. You know, it's all "government issue." And it's expensive to be a re-enactor. It's a lot more expensive than back in the day. That's why everyone wants to be a Reb. That's why there are so many Rebs out here. The romanticism of the Lost Cause, as it was, draws people to it.

You've got to do it to put on the show to educate these people who don't even know when the Civil War was fought. I think if you took people in the street, if I picked out twenty people for you, I'd lay even odds ten of them couldn't say within ten years when the Civil War was, and would have no other knowledge of it, except that's when the slaves were set free. That's about it; it's all they would know about it. It's kind of pathetic. But to come out here and actually put on the show for the tourists, and I think to a large extent a lot of the tourists are already Civil War buffs. I doubt if you get many totally cold fish that are just out here because there is nothing else to do that day. They come out here to see a Civil War battle so they usually have a little bit of knowledge already. It is a slug-fest just to get to one of these big events as a spectator because all the roads are clogged and you have to walk like a mile just to see the battle and all that. So there is a little dedication among the spectators. We're really aiming at the younger crowd, which everyone is griping about, which is off in the video games. Well rather than gripe, we try to get them out here, to have their hands on something real, and to see and feel it, to tell them the little stories."

Private William M. Irwin

Private William M. Irwin was born in [Guilford County] and was by occupation a ginner prior to enlisting at age 26, February 22, 1862. Wounded at Mechanicsville, Virginia, June 26, 1862. Court-martialed on March 6, 1863. Reason he was court-martialed not reported. Wounded at Chancellorsville, Virginia, May 1-3, 1863. Deserted in June, 1863, but returned to duty prior to July 3, 1863, when he was wounded and captured at Gettysburg, Pennsylvania. Confined at Fort Delaware, Delaware, until released on or about September 22, 1863, after joining the U.S. Army. Assigned to Company G, 3rd Regiment Maryland Cavalry.

John Sheehan, private, age 57, for 23 years a crew-chief of tree-climbers for the Teamsters Union, and since 1996, having earned the first terminal degree in his family's history, has been a history professor.

"I was born in the South Bronx, New York City, to the children of four Irish immigrants. I hail from a heritage of sharecroppers on the lands of ethnically different landowners, whose generations had survived dispossession and Famine. My grandfather fought as a guerrilla with Eamon DeValera in the War of Independence that left Ireland sundered into a North and a South, with their peculiar cultural sensitivities. After losing the ensuing Civil War to rectify that situation, my maternal grandfather spearheaded the clannish exodus to America. All four grandparents gaped at Lady Liberty en route to the Ellis Island experience. As a result, I understand, albeit imperfectly, some of the cultural sensitivities of denizens of that union dubbed the United States of America. My father fought in France, the Battle of the Bulge, and Germany as a seventeen-year-old, and was personally responsible for reducing the ranks of the Master Race by a few. Some would dub him part of the "Greatest Generation" for their own agendas; I believe he returned as a highly functional soul suffering from Post-traumatic stress syndrome. I do know that he understood the ethereal notion of brotherhood and sacrifice. Whose "American" was he, I often ponder? I undertook this project as an offshoot of my study of an infamous Union Corps Commander at the Battle of Gettysburg, Dan Sickles. I particularly wanted to understand why Lee's hitherto successful Grand Tactics unraveled so badly at the particular topography allotted to Sickles south of that town. I wanted to experience the smoke, the chaos, the confusion, the adrenaline, and the camaraderie of such a martial experience. I admit to ancillary motives other than historical in this. Through a re-enactor acquaintance I was extended a gracious invitation by Ken Snyder to embed with the 22nd North Carolina for this experience. After my first encounter with drilling and shooting on the ground, I formulated, along with my colleague Keith Millman, a desire to learn why modern Americans re-enact. The result is this publication.

This project tiptoes on America's cultural sensitivities. I wonder, what is it I am a part of promoting? Do we construct our own Sociological Imaginations and those of others in our own images? Ah, the old rub of cultural relativism versus ethnocentrism. Does immersion in a culture of harmonicas, banjos, and barbecue force me into any politicized camp? I must admit that I struggled with the sensitive issues of extremist collective guilt and collective judgment with this project, but was determined to let men and women tell their stories solely for the purposes of true democratic principles. I also admit that I had a lot of fun with those fella's and ladies."

Private Samuel A. Pegram

Private Samuel A. Pegram enlisted in Guilford County at age 25, March 17, 1863, for the war. Wounded in the back and left arm at Chancellorsville, Virginia, May 1-4, 1863. Returned to duty on June 16, 1863. Wounded on July 1-3, 1863 at Gettysburg, Pennsylvania, where he "acted bravely." Wounded in the left leg at Reams' Station, Virginia, August 25, 1864. Left leg amputated. Died in hospital at Petersburg, Virginia, September 29, 1864, of wounds and/or "pneumonia."

Kevin Posey, private, age 49, is from St. Simon's Island, Georgia. He is in the plumbing business.

"I've been a re-enactor for twelve years. One reason is family. I want to honor General Frazier. He's my fifth or sixth great uncle. He was mortally wounded in battle and died on November 14th, 1863. He was from Wilkinson County, Mississippi. I'm also related to General Carnot Posey, who led one of Confederate brigades here at the Battle of Gettysburg. I'm here today to honor them.

I also re-enact just to make right the history of the Southern people, and the country. There's so much now a days where everything is supposed to be so politically correct that makes our history askew and makes it wrong; so re-enacting is my small part to make that stay the course and be right. I want to educate those who, for one reason or another, aren't familiar with the historical aspect of a certain way of life, the way the war ran. The life of the Confederate soldier pretty much mirrored the life of a Union soldier. I've been studying the Civil War my whole life. To be able to pass this on to other people, to see the wide-eyed children enjoying it and striking home with the stories of how the men lived, the weight of the weapon, and everything, gives me great satisfaction. I want people to know the exact cause of the Civil War. It's preposterous nowadays, if you listen to it. It's one hundred percent about slavery and nothing else, and that's not proper, that's not correct. People remember Lincoln as the big emancipator, but few people realize that Lincoln was one of the greatest racists this country has ever seen. He was willing to let the southern states come back into the Union, even with keeping their slaves. He thought that the black race was an inferior race. It was his general idea at one time to also try and ship them all off somewhere. The northern populace, as a whole, could have cared less about slavery. In fact, there were just as many, if not more people in the North that were against the black man. They just didn't want them to be slaves; they thought that was wrong. But they didn't want them living with them either. Free the black man, but don't let him come live with us. Another important thing is States' Rights. The South believed in state-run state government. For instance, New York Harbor could afford to pay more money to the sailors coming from Europe than say Charleston would, so the sailors naturally want to drop their goods in New York. Then, middle men, coming from New York down to Charleston are going to levy a tax on those items, and so this stuff that started to cost, say twenty bucks a barrel or whatever, by the time it gets to Charleston, it costs eighty bucks or more. Guys from Charleston wanted the right to say, "we trade with Europe our way, and you trade your way. Don't beat us out of our money twice." The right for states to come up with their own determination of what's right and what's wrong is what the Constitution says."

61

Private Robert W. Bolton

Private Robert W. Bolton resided in Caswell County where he enlisted on February 1, 1862. Reported absent wounded in October 1862. Place and date wounded not reported. Returned to duty on an unspecified date. Wounded at Gettysburg, Pennsylvania, July 3, 1863. Returned to duty on or about November 27, 1863. Wounded at the Jerusalem Plank Road near Petersburg, Virginia, June 23, 1864. Returned to duty prior to November 1, 1864. No further records.

Michael Breedlove, private, age 63, was born in Missouri, and currently resides in Columbia, Missouri. Recently retired, he was a geographer by profession.

"I have been a re-enactor for four years, ever since I moved back from the West. I re-enact because I discovered that I had 8 relatives that served with the 22nd North Carolina. I started out looking through the National Parks service records for Breedloves by state, and then into each unit. I went through numerous folders for each person, extracting their actual service records and compiling them. I've seen their Confederate service records for each one of them. I do believe re-enactments serve a purpose. I am a true believer that the true story of the history of the South is not being reflected in the history books served up to the children of today. And, in as much, some of that history can actually be shown perhaps through re-enactments or interaction with the public I think that is a good thing.

Beyond that, I think, personally, I try to get a sense of place and time; it is hard to get, but occasionally you perhaps get a feel of what it might have been like to have lived then, even though you know you're not there. There's a certain interaction with people with similar interests, a search for a certain place and time. And as long as my body will allow it, I enjoy the camaraderie among other things. There's a sense of commonality in many ways with re-enactors that's just fun. I like to call them Southern Boy Scouts with guns. In this particular case I searched out the colonel of the 22nd because I found relatives that had served with it and I specifically wanted to re-enact where I could actually be here as a personal honor to my relatives, and to give my son Andrew, perhaps, a sense of place too. I just really enjoy the people I re-enact with. I always learn something new and that's a good thing."

Private John Mains

Private John Mains resided in Alleghany County where he enlisted at age 20, May 27, 1861. Wounded at Seven Pines, Virginia May 31, 1861. Returned to duty on an unspecified date. Killed at Gettysburg, Pennsylvania, July 2, 1863.

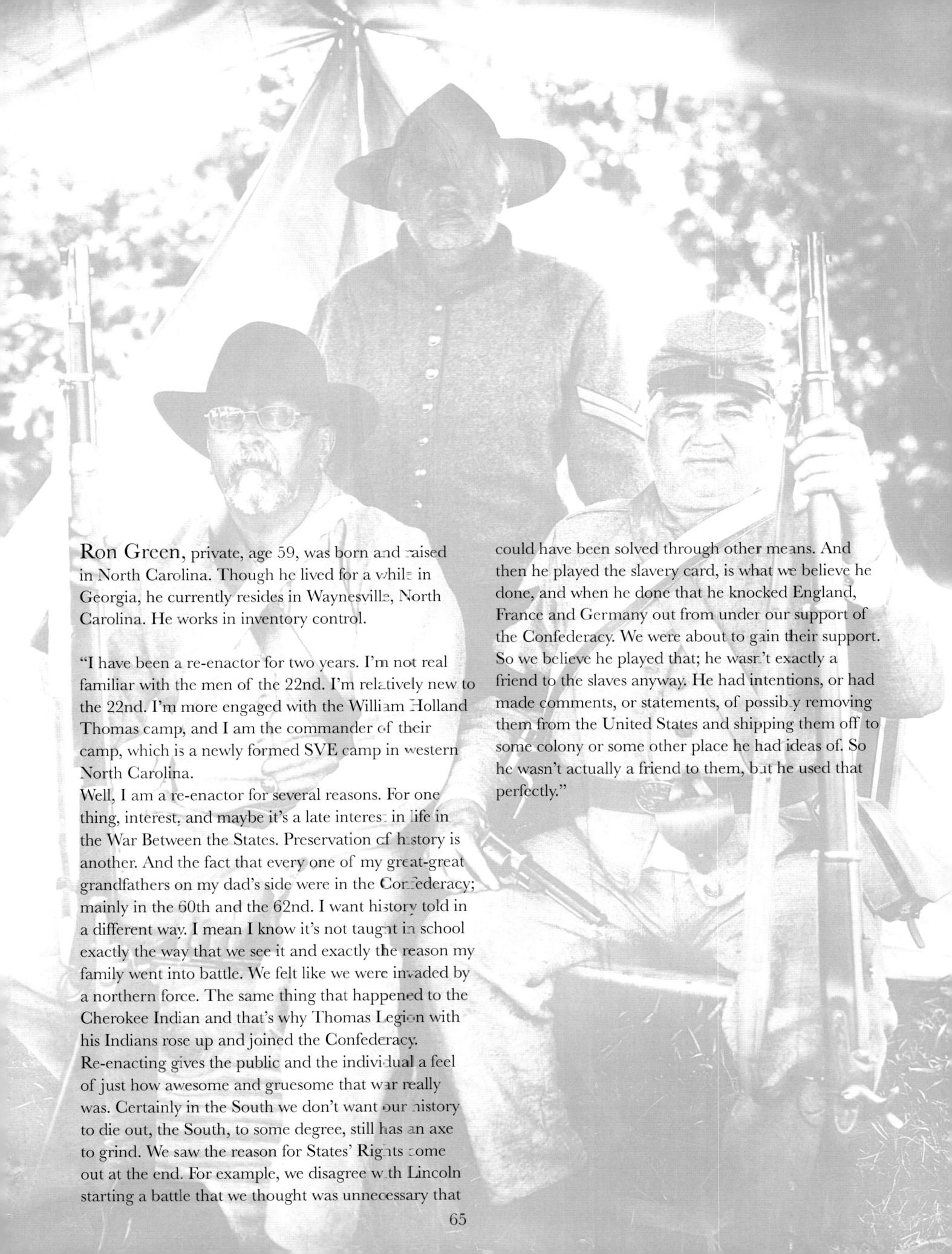

Ron Green, private, age 59, was born and raised in North Carolina. Though he lived for a while in Georgia, he currently resides in Waynesville, North Carolina. He works in inventory control.

"I have been a re-enactor for two years. I'm not real familiar with the men of the 22nd. I'm relatively new to the 22nd. I'm more engaged with the William Holland Thomas camp, and I am the commander of their camp, which is a newly formed SVE camp in western North Carolina.

Well, I am a re-enactor for several reasons. For one thing, interest, and maybe it's a late interest in life in the War Between the States. Preservation of history is another. And the fact that every one of my great-great grandfathers on my dad's side were in the Confederacy; mainly in the 60th and the 62nd. I want history told in a different way. I mean I know it's not taught in school exactly the way that we see it and exactly the reason my family went into battle. We felt like we were invaded by a northern force. The same thing that happened to the Cherokee Indian and that's why Thomas Legion with his Indians rose up and joined the Confederacy. Re-enacting gives the public and the individual a feel of just how awesome and gruesome that war really was. Certainly in the South we don't want our history to die out, the South, to some degree, still has an axe to grind. We saw the reason for States' Rights come out at the end. For example, we disagree with Lincoln starting a battle that we thought was unnecessary that could have been solved through other means. And then he played the slavery card, is what we believe he done, and when he done that he knocked England, France and Germany out from under our support of the Confederacy. We were about to gain their support. So we believe he played that; he wasn't exactly a friend to the slaves anyway. He had intentions, or had made comments, or statements, of possibly removing them from the United States and shipping them off to some colony or some other place he had ideas of. So he wasn't actually a friend to them, but he used that perfectly."

65

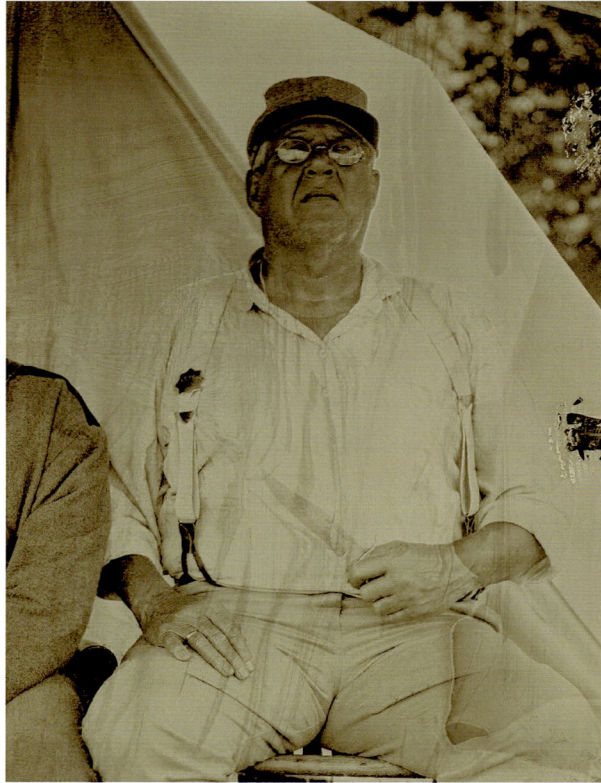

Private Randy V. Taylor

Private Randy V. Taylor resided in Caldwell County where he enlisted at age 25, March 19, 1862. Captured at or near Chancellorsville, Virginia, on or about May 1-3, 1863. Paroled on May 4, 1863. Captured at Gettysburg, Pennsylvania, July 3-4, 1863. Confined at Fort Delaware, Delaware, until paroled and transferred to City Point, Virginia, where he was received August 1, 1863 for exchange. Returned to duty on an unspecified date. Hospitalized at Richmond, Virginia, January 29, 1864, with typhoid fever and returned to duty on February 17, 1864. No further records.

James Vernon Carter, private, age 66, was born in Burnsville, North Carolina and lives there to this day. He is a retired police officer and currently works in a secondary school as a teacher of music and history.

"I have been a re-enactor for five years. I just happened upon the 22nd North Carolina when I moved to Carolina when I retired in 2008. I always wanted to do re-enacting, but because of my profession I wasn't free on weekends for years and this finally gave me the opportunity to do it. Luckily, I stumbled onto the 22nd and they are probably the best unit I've ever seen as far as the dedication, camaraderie, and the commitment to learning the battles and history. What had begun out of curiosity grew into a personal quest for information about relatives. I had relatives in the Civil War. I had several, my great-great grandfather and his brothers enlisted in the 27th North Carolina in Leonor County. They were wounded in Sharpsburg. They were wounded in Newberg. They recuperated and returned to duty and finished the war. They had moved out to Texas after the war and subsequently on to Louisiana, were my father was born. And they were also in the 3rd artillery battalion I'm told, and they were here as well. Well, I think for everyone, re-enacting gives them a sense, especially if they had relatives, of where they came from, and the culture they came from. It preserves and honors hallowed ground and personnel that lost their lives in the war; and we have preservation organizations within re-enactor groups, and the SVE, that strive and they preserve the battlefields. They preserve monuments. They prevent encroachment of businesses and corporations that want to build on the battlegrounds and we're all tied into that. There are thousands of us and we are strong in numbers and that's what we want to propagate. We want to keep this going. I'm sixty-six and I'm not really infirm, but I can't run across the field like Julie Andrews in the "Sound of Music" any more. So we expect the young ones to take the reins, but they've got to be taught; we have to teach them. We do that by example. Lectures are fine, but actually going to the battlefields, the sites of what happened, you can't beat that. And when you go for the first time, it's just overwhelming. There are big places, big places like Gettysburg, Vicksburg, Chattanooga, Shiloh, places like that you get a certain feeling. And Gettysburg is a special place because even when you go through certain areas you'll get a presence. The hair will stand up on the back of your neck."

Private John P. Stack

Private John P. Stack enlisted in Guilford County at age 28, February 22, 1862. Wounded in both legs at Seven Pines, Virginia, May 31, 1862. Wounded in the right thigh and captured at Gettysburg, Pennsylvania, July 1-3, 1863. Confined at various Federal hospitals until transferred to Point Lookout, Maryland, October 15-18, 1863. Confined at Point Lookout until paroled and transferred for exchange on or about September 30, 1864. Company records do not indicate whether he returned to duty; however, he was paroled at Greensboro on May 10, 1865.

Kevin Jefferson, private, age 60, was born in Palo Alto, Pennsylvania and currently lives in Pottsville, Pennsylvania.

"For many years, I've been looking for a home, not only a comfortable place to live, but a home in my heart, where I can be with people who care. I have family down in North Carolina, and my wife is a Native American, so I have been looking at the points of view of many different people for many different years, trying to figure things out. I looked at Civil War re-enactors as part of this process, and I ran into Ken Snyder. Ken said want to join us, and I joined. All things seem to come together: learning history from different perspectives, while living it, and finding a good home with my fellow re-enactors."

Private John Haney

Private John Haney resided in McDowell County where he enlisted at age 46, April 15, 1862. Captured by the enemy on an unspecified date and was hospitalized in a Federal hospital at Alexandria, Virginia, September 5, 1862. Exchanged prior to October 1, 1862. Returned to duty on an unspecified date. Captured at Gettysburg, Pennsylvania, July 3, 1863. Confined at Fort Delaware, Delaware, until transferred to Point Lookout, Maryland, October 15-18, 1863. Confined at Point Lookout, Maryland, October 15-18, 1863 until paroled and transferred to Boulware's and Cox's Wharves, James River, Virginia, February 20-21, 1865, for exchange.

Gary Rath, private, age 62, has lived in Chatham, Virginia, near the North Carolina border, and currently lives in Gettysburg, Pennsylvania, in a barn one mile south of the battlefield. He is a public school teacher and a coach.

"I have been a re-enactor for twenty-two years. I've always been interested in medicine and medical history. That led me to Civil War history and its medical practices. They were horrifying. This led me to want to see the big picture of the Civil War, to study it on a more intense level. I want to educate the public about it. I want to keep history alive. Ever since the invention of I-phones, history has been de-emphasized; but it's so important. Soldiers in the Civil War knew the Three R's: Readin', Ritin', and 'Rithmatic. College students today don't even know the Three R's. History is not like any other subject. It's about morals; it's about decisions. It's really important. That's why I re-enact. I like to talk to the public and show them how important their history is, and I do it through public school programs also. But, to tell you the truth, I do it too, because I love the camaraderie. It's fun."

Private Benjamin Franklin Roberts

Private Benjamin Franklin Roberts was born in Chatham County and was by occupation a miner prior to enlisting in Guilford County at age 23, May 23, 1861. Captured by the enemy in an unspecified battle and was confined at Fort Monroe, Virginia. Paroled and transferred to Aiken's Landing, James River, Virginia, where he was received September 7, 1862, for exchange. Declared exchanged at Aiken's Landing on September 21, 1862. Returned to duty on an unspecified date. Wounded and captured at Gettysburg, Pennsylvania, July 3-5, 1863. Confined at Fort Delaware, Delaware, until released on or about October 4, 1863, after joining the U.S. Army. Assigned to Company G, 1st regiment Connecticut Cavalry.

Keith Zelinski, private, age 37, lives in Hempstead, Maryland. He is a business owner.

"I was introduced in high school to a unit, and after serving in the actual army, I came to the 22nd a few years ago.

Well for me history is important. I've been a living historian since I was a child. The Civil War is my favorite period. When I look at the problems that we face today the same issues that plagued us one hundred and fifty years ago are still facing us today. And I want to teach and educate the public because the conquerors write the history books for us all. I want to get a better understanding of why these boys fought. I mean I know, but with every event that I do, and every battle that I engage in, I understand more and more that it was a war for independence. And I want to pay tribute to and honor those men that went before me.

Re-enacting is important. There are a lot of older men that do this. The Younger generation needs to step up. If you look at our culture, our society, our government, most people don't give a damn about what's going on. Men that re-enact, we do. We care about this country. We care about our constitution, about words like honor and integrity. They mean things; they're not words on a page to us. I think most every man here has personal honor, on both sides, North and South. It doesn't matter. We're old souls, I'd like to say. I'd like to think we're old souls. Well, I feel that I was born in the wrong time period. I think the reason that I'm here is to remind people of the past and where we came from, so we don't lose our way

I had relatives on both sides…. It's really emotional…. I don't know why I've always been passionate about the military and soldiers. I come from a military family. We have served in just about every war, from the War of 1812 onward; somebody in my family has served this country. So for me, joining the military comes from the heart. I can never repay those boys for what they did. I mean my brother. Ow. I feel like I haven't done enough, even though I served, I haven't done enough. I don't think I can ever do enough…. Sorry…. It's powerful. If you can't shed tears for what you're passionate about, then you haven't lived. So it's okay to be passionate. It's just that men died for a way of life."

Private Marshall S. Ranes

Private Marshall S. Ranes was born in Randolph County where he resided as a farmer prior to enlisting in Randolph County at age 19, June 10, 1861. Wounded in the foot at the second battle of Manassas, Virginia, August 30, 1862. Returned to duty on an unspecified date. Captured at or near Gettysburg, Pennsylvania, July 3-5, 1863. Confined at Fort Delaware, Delaware, until transferred to Point Lookout, Maryland, October 15-18, 1863. Released on January 26, 1864 after joining the U.S. Army. Assigned to Company B, 1st Regiment U.S. Volunteer Infantry.

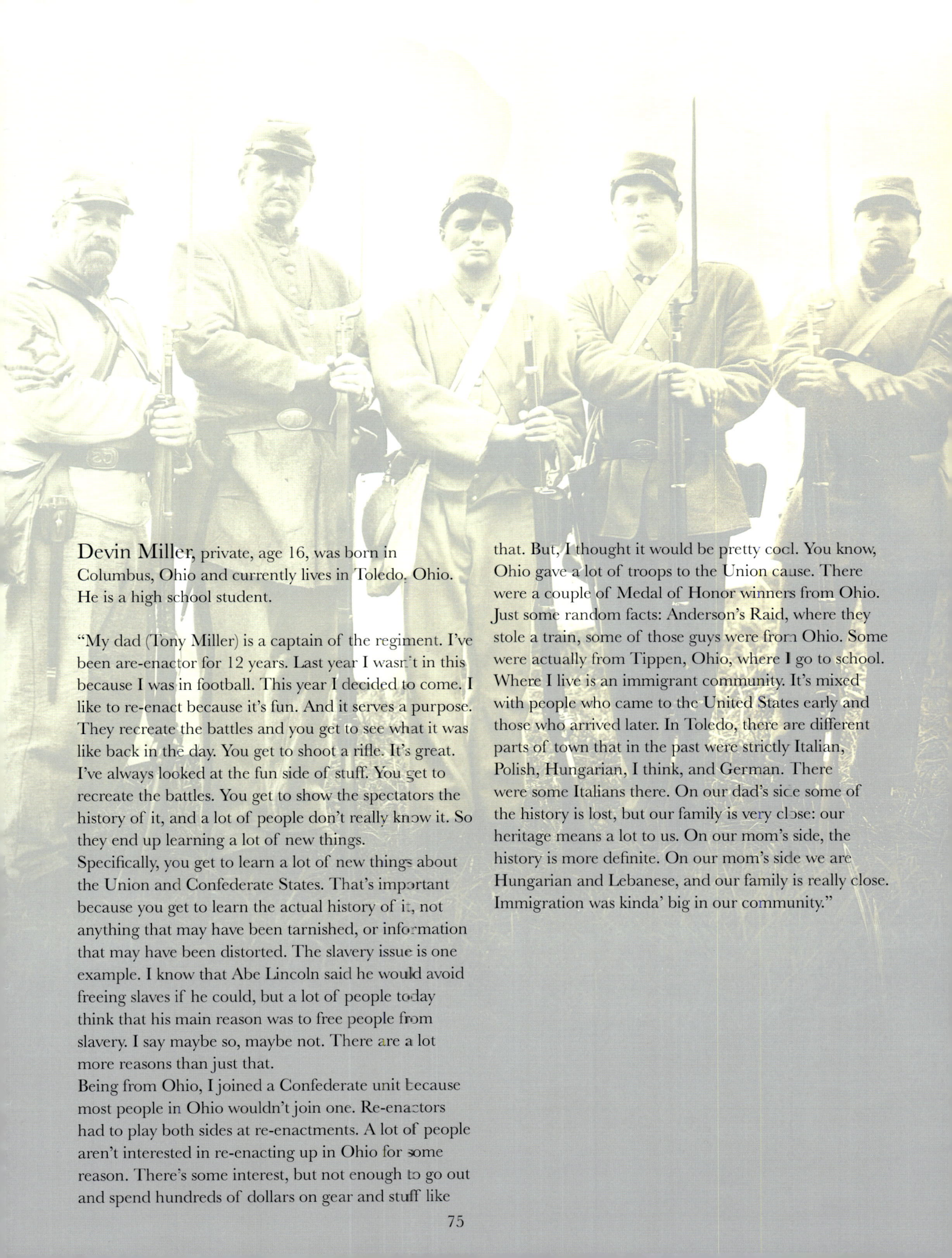

Devin Miller, private, age 16, was born in Columbus, Ohio and currently lives in Toledo. Ohio. He is a high school student.

"My dad (Tony Miller) is a captain of the regiment. I've been are-enactor for 12 years. Last year I wasn't in this because I was in football. This year I decided to come. I like to re-enact because it's fun. And it serves a purpose. They recreate the battles and you get to see what it was like back in the day. You get to shoot a rifle. It's great. I've always looked at the fun side of stuff. You get to recreate the battles. You get to show the spectators the history of it, and a lot of people don't really know it. So they end up learning a lot of new things.
Specifically, you get to learn a lot of new things about the Union and Confederate States. That's important because you get to learn the actual history of it, not anything that may have been tarnished, or information that may have been distorted. The slavery issue is one example. I know that Abe Lincoln said he would avoid freeing slaves if he could, but a lot of people today think that his main reason was to free people from slavery. I say maybe so, maybe not. There are a lot more reasons than just that.
Being from Ohio, I joined a Confederate unit because most people in Ohio wouldn't join one. Re-enactors had to play both sides at re-enactments. A lot of people aren't interested in re-enacting up in Ohio for some reason. There's some interest, but not enough to go out and spend hundreds of dollars on gear and stuff like

that. But, I thought it would be pretty cool. You know, Ohio gave a lot of troops to the Union cause. There were a couple of Medal of Honor winners from Ohio. Just some random facts: Anderson's Raid, where they stole a train, some of those guys were from Ohio. Some were actually from Tippen, Ohio, where I go to school. Where I live is an immigrant community. It's mixed with people who came to the United States early and those who arrived later. In Toledo, there are different parts of town that in the past were strictly Italian, Polish, Hungarian, I think, and German. There were some Italians there. On our dad's side some of the history is lost, but our family is very close: our heritage means a lot to us. On our mom's side, the history is more definite. On our mom's side we are Hungarian and Lebanese, and our family is really close. Immigration was kinda' big in our community."

Private E.P. Miller, Jr.

Private E.P. Miller, Jr. resided in Caldwell County where he enlisted at age 19, April 30, 1861. Transferred to Company M of this regiment subsequent to August 31, 1861, but was transferred back to this company in July, 1862, while absent from wounds received at Seven Pines, Virginia, May 31, 1862. Reported absent without leave in September 1862. Returned to duty prior to July 3-5, 1863, when he wounded and captured at Gettysburg, Pennsylvania. Confined at Fort Delaware, Delaware, until transferred to Point Lookout, Maryland, October 15-18, 1863. Confined at Point Lookout until paroled and transferred to Boulware's and Cox's Wharves, James River, Virginia, February 18, 1865, for exchange. Reported present with a detachment of paroled and exchanged prisoners at Camp Lee, near Richmond, Virginia, February 23, 1865.

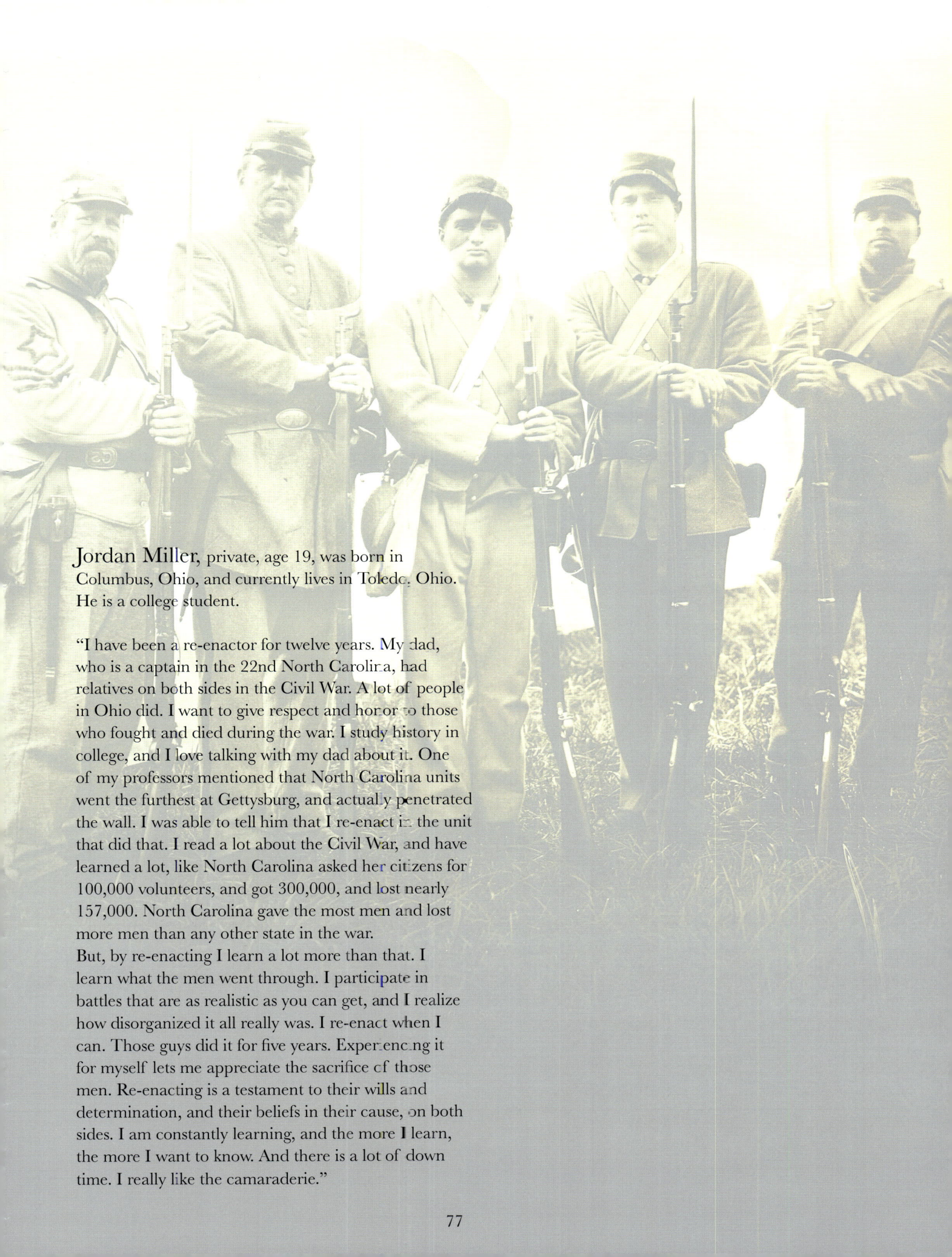

Jordan Miller, private, age 19, was born in
Columbus, Ohio, and currently lives in Toledo, Ohio.
He is a college student.

"I have been a re-enactor for twelve years. My dad,
who is a captain in the 22nd North Carolina, had
relatives on both sides in the Civil War. A lot of people
in Ohio did. I want to give respect and honor to those
who fought and died during the war. I study history in
college, and I love talking with my dad about it. One
of my professors mentioned that North Carolina units
went the furthest at Gettysburg, and actually penetrated
the wall. I was able to tell him that I re-enact in the unit
that did that. I read a lot about the Civil War, and have
learned a lot, like North Carolina asked her citizens for
100,000 volunteers, and got 300,000, and lost nearly
157,000. North Carolina gave the most men and lost
more men than any other state in the war.
But, by re-enacting I learn a lot more than that. I
learn what the men went through. I participate in
battles that are as realistic as you can get, and I realize
how disorganized it all really was. I re-enact when I
can. Those guys did it for five years. Experiencing it
for myself lets me appreciate the sacrifice of those
men. Re-enacting is a testament to their wills and
determination, and their beliefs in their cause, on both
sides. I am constantly learning, and the more I learn,
the more I want to know. And there is a lot of down
time. I really like the camaraderie."

Private Durant W. Busick

Private Durant W. Busick was born in Rockingham County and rsided in Guilford County where he was by occupation a farmer prior to enlisting in Guilford County at age 18, May 23, 1861. Wounded in the left knee at Frayser's Farm, Virginia, June 30, 1862. Reported absent wounded through October 1862. Returned to duty on an unspecified date. Wounded in the left leg and captured at Gettysburg, Pennsylvania, July 1-4, 1863. Left leg amputated. Hospitalized at David's Island, New York Harbor, until paroled and transferred to City Point, Virginia where he was received September 16, 1863, for exchange. Retired to the Invalid Corps on August 24, 1864. Paroled at Greensboro in 1865.

Christopher Brang, private, age 17, was born and raised in Mercersburg, Pennsylvania. He is currently attending high school and hopes to pursue a career with the railroad.

"I've been a re-enactor for nine years. Drawn to an interest in the railroad, friends of mine drew me into an interest in re-enacting. Since then I love doing it. It's a great hobby, at the same time it's also a nice way to honor those who went before and sacrificed their lives for what they believed in.

Re-enactment serves a purpose. It tells the story of those who went before us. It's kind of hard to put into words. I like to joke around a lot that I was born in the wrong century. I should have been born 150 – 160 years ago. It's a time period that I love, really. Sometimes you feel like you're not alone out there. You might feel like those guys are with you.

Yes, it's taught me quite a lot. If you don't know your history you're bound to repeat it. I love connecting with people. I also belong to several other units that I re-enact with and definitely with those units I'm closer with some of the people. This unit, I'm half connected with people in the 22nd, but I like making new friends."

Private Lawrence Austin

Private Lawrence Austin was born in Randolph County where he resided as a farmer prior to enlisting in Randolph County at age 16, March 6, 1862. Wounded in the side at the second battle of Manassas, Virginia, August 29, 1862. Captured at or near Gettysburg, Pennsylvania July 1-5, 1863. Confined at Fort Delaware, Delaware, until transferred to Point Lookout, Maryland, October 15-18, 1863. Paroled at Point Lookout and transferred to Cox's Landing, James River, Virginia where he was received February 14-15, 1865 for exchange.

Joseph Rathbone, private, age 14, was born, and lives, in Canton, North Carolina. He is a student in school.

"I have been a re-enactor for five years. I got started because my dad is the captain and so he brought me into it. Once I did it once, I got hooked. I love to shoot and I love to be with all these other guys. Talking around the fire is always good fun. Telling stories, all that stuff.

I know a little bit about the 22nd North Carolina regiment. I know they come out of McDowell County, primarily. I know I had family in the Thomas Legion, I do know that. My four great grandfathers were in the war. I believe one was in the 29th North Carolina, Company and he was killed. He was part of the home guard.

Re-enactments preserve the history and what actually happened. It helps to show people who never knew any of this what it really was like, and it puts everything into perspective. It's a great example of what it was truly like. Mostly, I really like all the history lessons and stories we tell around the fire. I've learned so much just sitting there talking than I learned in school. I mean I really do, I love it. It's great."

Chaplain F. H. Wood

Chaplain F. H. Wood was appointed in February 1863. Present or accounted for through October 1864.

Wayne W Justice, chaplain, age 70, was born in Buffalo, New York, and has lived in North Carolina for twenty eight years. He owns a small auto repair shop.

"I have been a re-enactor for eight years, and I portray the regimental chaplain. I joined the 22nd North Carolina because my great-great grandfather served with Thomas's Legion out of Waynesville, NC. Even though I was born in Buffalo, New York, or outside of Buffalo, my father and his family were from North Carolina. In fact, the family had been in North Carolina since the 1660's; so my family is from there. The main reason my father went to Buffalo was to look for work. But, I came back, my father came back, my brothers came back, everybody came back. I really enjoy re-enacting. I enjoy keeping the history alive, plus, I enjoy the camaraderie with the re-enactors. Re-enactments definitely serve a purpose. They keep the history alive. And I think they serve to portray some of the true story. It's not really told in our history books. Well, many things that are in our history books are not exactly true. Or the truth has been screwed with a little bit. Someone said the victors get to write the history. That's right. Confederate General Patrick Cleburne said: "if we do not win the war the history will be written by the northern side and our schools will teach the northern point of view."
We explain a lot about what actually happened in the fields and what differences there were in the actual involvement of the troops compared to what might be said, because often times I think the Confederate Army was construed as a bunch of rebels. Actually, they were a very well organized force. The official name was the "War of the Rebellion" for Congress. And the Emancipation Proclamation was extremely unpopular with both the North and the South. In fact, more with the North than with the South. Lincoln also said that if anybody talked against it, they would be arrested and imprisoned. Finally, you'll never hear this anywhere else, but 6-7% of the Confederate army held slaves. Do you seriously think 93-94% of the Confederate Army was fighting for slavery? Even if you use the counter argument that in the northern, upper south, approximately 25% of the households held some slaves, most households didn't have very many at all. Again, you're still talking about 75% of those who served had no personal vested interest in slavery. In fact, most men were fighting to defend their homes from invasion. That's all they wanted. They invaded us. My theory on that, truthfully is, Lee never really wanted to win the war; he only wanted the North to say: "Okay, just leave them alone.""

Leslie Brang (contemporary)

Leslie Brang, age 60, was born in Baltimore, Maryland and currently lives in Mercersburg, Pennsylvania. She is a school bus driver.

"I have been a re-enactor for five years. I re-enact with the 22nd North Carolina because right after graduating from high school, my first husband, who was in the Marine Corps, was stationed in Jacksonville, North Carolina. We lived there for two years, and I loved it. I also re-enact for the passion. The Civil War was the most important, or at least the second most important, period in American history, second, if anything, only to the Revolution. And it is a period of time that has been so ill represented in our education system. When I was coming through high school, this era was not taught in its proper context. It was taught that this was strictly a racial issue that was started over a couple of contrary states in the South not wanting to give up their slaves and their luxuries. It was about much more than that. I grew up hearing that the generation of World War II was the greatest generation, but as I am learning more, I am convinced that the generation of the Civil War was the greatest generation because there was so much political conflict. This was a fledgling country. It had so many growing pains to go through, and there are so many opinions about that. But, for those opinions to mean something they have to be backed up by something, something real. Those opinions were met face to face on battlefields, every day. All the South wanted was the right to make certain decisions within the individual states. It wanted a level of government that was under the federal level and only basically within that level, but it recognized that the states needed to be able to govern themselves within certain parameters outside of the federal level. That's what it was about. Slavery was a prime issue, but it was not the only issue by any means. What do we have today? We have three levels of government: the federal level, the state level, and the local level. All three levels interact, but yet have their separate parameters under which they can operate. That is because of the Civil War. The South may have lost the war, but we won because we established that the states do have the right to govern themselves within certain parameters, and that's all it was asking for in the first place. That's not what our textbooks have been teaching us. But, if you put it into perspective, that's what we learned. But, we would never be able to look at that perspective if it weren't for re-enactors who come out here and embrace the bits of information that are now coming forth. They had ancestors who fought. Some of this documentation is within their families. They know who the heck they are; they know who their ancestors were. Many of them portray their ancestors. Many of them join the units that their ancestors originally belonged to, the representative units. We got a bunch of them. To them this is not a weekend hobby. This is a passion. This is them allowing their ancestors a voice and an opportunity to re-teach American history the way it happened."

Wendy Davis (contemporary)

Wendy Davis, age 34, lives in Hampstead, Maryland. She is an Owner/Service Tech for the Cornerstone Cleaning Company.

"I have been a re-enactor for four years because this era has just always really fascinated me, everything about it, every aspect. It's not just entertainment to me; I'm here for the people, to teach them. They need to learn this; they need to see this. I wish more of the people would interact with us and ask us questions so they could become a little more educated and not just entertained. Re-enacting is very important. I think we're keeping this whole thing alive. I mean, if it wasn't for people like us, then this would die off and the younger generation would have absolutely no clue about any of this. They wouldn't know anything about the battles. They wouldn't know anything about the men leading the troops. They would know nothing about the way the people lived, the way they dressed, any of it. Remembering this is important because it made us who we are today. You need to know where you came from before you can move on, to go forward.

I legitimately like talking to people who come to watch the battles and I want to interact with people. I like to give them a little piece of what I know, and help to educate people. And the people respond pretty well usually. They seem very interested. They seem very into what I have to say, what I'm talking to them about. They definitely ask a lot of questions; sometimes it seems like I have a little bit more of a different perspective on things when I talk to them. I also use to do tours in town here, in Gettysburg. I used to love to talk to people afterwards because they would just ask so many questions. And it really seemed like it shed a light on certain things for them. It was almost like giving them a little behind the scenes kind of information, little side notes that maybe they couldn't get out of a book, couldn't get off of a program. I did that for about two and a half years."

POSTSCRIPT

There is a great value in experiencing other people re-living history. Re-enactments make history come alive in a continuous way through the re-enactors lives, their personal histories, their understanding of politics, the knowledge of the war, the intensity of being immersed in a battle on a historic field, and their relationships with each other. The diversity of ideas, as well as the rich passions of the men and women of the 22nd North Carolina Infantry Regiment, were all focused in the actual preparation for, and the clamor of, the re-enacted battle.

The project makes available through the tintypes and the voices of the participants a view into one of the most important historical events in American history, and allows us to see that history through the lens of the Immortal Imagination.

What had started out as an exercise to understand better why Robert E. Lee's attacks at Gettysburg had unraveled so disastrously on the heels of some of the Confederacy's greatest victories, became a project that delved into the heart of what it means to be an American in the 21st Century. Having camped, drilled, marched, dined, and re-enacted with the men and women of the 22nd North Carolina Infantry Regiment was gratifying and enriching in and of itself. But more importantly, having talked with and listened to the stories and lives of these people, as Americans with their own particular views, made us reflect on how remarkable this experiment in American Democracy truly is. We, as a people, continually re-make and re-define ourselves. To look back at the Civil War from our various political vantage points today makes some people unable to see the history of the United States and the factors that influenced that history from the points of view of the participants at the time. It is only by doing that, that one can best judge how they lived and died according to the accepted values of their generation. The war was fought to change those values in the crucible of battle, and they have shifted several times since then. Recently, the tragic racially-based shootings, on June 17, 2015 at the Emanuel African Methodist Episcopal Church in Charleston, South Carolina, has prompted the state legislature of South Carolina to order the removal of the flag of the Confederacy from the state capitol grounds. As a result of these events, the place that the Civil War occupies in the Immortal Imagination is on the verge of being re-mythologized once again. It is more imperative than ever for the idea of the Immortal Imagination to be understood by Americans living in every region of the United States. The call for "putting that flag in a museum" is actually a call that should put re-enacting, as an interactive "museum" of "living history," on a vital and respected activity for teaching Americans who they really are and where they have come from. The story of America is a great story and it is composed of many characters and many voices.

INDEX